Time-Span Quilts

BY

BECKY HERDLE

Time-Span Quilts

BY

BECKY HERDLE

American Quilter's Society

P. O. Box 3290 • Paducah, KY 42002-3290

Library of Congress Cataloging-in-Publication Data

Herdle, Becky.
    Time-span quilts : new quilts from old tops / by Becky Herdle.
        p.   cm.
    Includes bibliographical references (p.   ) and indexes.
    ISBN 0-89145 -845-X : $16.95
    1. Quilts--Repairing.   2. Quilts--Conservation and restoration.
3. Quilting.   I Title.
TT835.H446   1994
746.46'0488--dc20

94--38002
CIP

Additional copies of this book may be ordered from:

American Quilter's Society
P.O. Box 3290
Paducah, KY 42002-3290
@16.95. Add $1.00 for postage and handling.

Copyright: 1994, Becky Herdle

Dedication

This book is dedicated to

LLOYD E. HERDLE

my loving husband and best friend.

His support throughout the years has enriched every aspect of my life, including the partnership we have enjoyed while raising six wonderful children.

Though not a quilter himself, he thoroughly understands and appreciates quilts; he has provided many excellent suggestions that have helped in my work; and he has tolerated without criticism the confusion involved in living with a quilter.

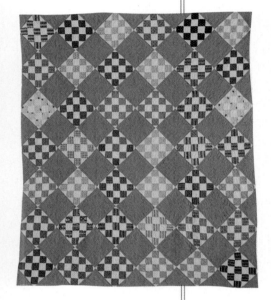

Photo Credit

A very special thank you to

ROBERT S. HARRIS

Photographer Extraordinaire

Without his efforts this book might never have been completed.

An accomplished career photographer, he has worked worldwide in more than sixty countries and in areas as diverse as filming coral reefs, ski races, and parachute jumps. His photographs have won numerous awards and top prizes in many contests.

Now retired and constantly busy as a lecturer, consultant, and photographer, his dedication to perfection has brought the quilts and quilt tops in this book to life.

All photographs in this book were taken by Robert S. Harris unless otherwise indicated.

Plate I-1. *(above)*
NINE-PATCH CHECKER-
BOARD, 63" x 75",
Time span: c. 1880–1993.
Hand pieced, hand quilted.
Top was from New Hampshire
with no known history. Quilt-
ed without change.

Acknowledgments

Thanks first of all to my husband, Lloyd, who has gone with me to auctions, flea markets, antique shows, and just about anywhere a quilt top might turn up; who has put up with a messy house loaded with quilts in all stages of completion; who has carried heavy loads of quilts many places for me; and who has tolerated my absence when I've deserted him to go to various locations to talk about my interest in Time-Span Quilts.

Thanks to my daughter, Beth, who has searched yard sales, flea markets, and antique shows from Georgia to California and found numerous tops for me.

Thanks to both my husband and my son, Ken, who have given me ideas and interesting suggestions for ways to quilt the tops – ways I would never have thought of on my own.

Thanks to Suzzy Payne, quiltmaking author and teacher, whose various classes caught my interest and inspired me to become involved in quilting.

Thanks to the friends who have quilted tops or shared their own Time-Span Quilts for use in this book: Lenore Harvey, Ruth Norton, Diane Crisafulli, Anna Farrell, Clara Pope, Joyce Wightman, and Helen Heckert.

Thanks to Carolyn Maruggi, a certified quilt appraiser and very good friend, who helped me with the dating of the tops photographed for use in this book.

Thanks to Florence Merritt, who shared with me her method for removing stains from antique quilts.

Thanks to Marie Geary and Jeanne Glenfield, directors of the Eastcoast Quilters Alliance in Westford, Massachusetts, for suggesting the use of the wonderfully descriptive name, "Time-Span Quilts," which I now use to describe all the new quilts from old tops that I make.

Thanks to Vicki Faoro, Elaine Wilson, Mary Jo Kurten, and the American Quilter's Society for their help in making this book become a reality.

Thanks to all those friends who have oohed and aahed when I showed them a completed quilt and thereby kept me believing in myself and the end products that I have so thoroughly enjoyed making.

Thanks to all the quilters (known or unknown) who made the original tops or blocks for the quilts in this book. I would like to think that they can see and are pleased with the way their efforts have turned out.

Table of Contents

Plate I-2. (right)
BROKEN DISHES,
72" x 84", Time span:
c. 1880–1983. Hand pieced,
hand quilted. The top was
made by Mrs. Hatch of
Waterloo, New York. A small,
extra border at one end was
removed and used to replace
two triangles in one block.
It was bound with a print
fabric.

Introduction

Over the years, a large number of quilt tops have been made and left unfinished, but it was quite by accident that they caught my interest.

In the late 1970's, my daughter and I made and sold a variety of small items in craft shows, including some patchwork pillows. At one show a woman approached me and asked if I was interested in buying a quilt top. I had only started quilting a year or so before and hardly knew what an old top would be like, but I did have enough sense to say, "Of course."

The next day she brought in two lovely tops, both of which were in mint condition. Her price to me seemed very high, and I was hesitant about such a purchase, but nevertheless I liked them so much that I bought them. Today I would recognize their value much more quickly and would not hesitate a moment.

In those days, because of the time needed to make things for our craft shows, I had little time to make new quilts of my own. I do all my piecing on the sewing machine, and my craft show work, which was also done by machine, took priority. But I've never liked to do machine work at night, so my evenings were left free for quilting. Soon, though, I ran out of tops I had pieced and found myself with nothing to quilt during evening hours.

That's when I thought of the quilt tops I had bought. No one told me that you weren't supposed to quilt old tops – that it might decrease their value – and I'm not sure I would have cared if they had told me. I saw the potential for beautiful finished quilts and the answer to my need for something to quilt, so I began. THE LADY OF THE LAKE and BROKEN DISHES quilts shown in *Plates I-2 and 1-1,* page 12, are the ones I made from those very first tops I bought at the craft show.

From that time on my interest in old tops mushroomed, and today the quilts I have completed from them make a sizeable collection. I have enjoyed finding and working with old tops and making "new" quilts from them. This book will explain my feelings about completing the work of others, the attitudes of others about finishing old tops, problems I have encountered while completing tops, and methods I have found successful for dealing with problems.

The quilts pictured throughout this book were completed from tops made at different times during a span of more than a hundred years and show the wide variety my friends and I have worked with. For the most part, there is no known history for the tops so most of the dates given were determined with the help of Carolyn Maruggi, a certified quilt appraiser. Because dating old quilts and tops is accurate only to within a period of about ten years, the dates listed for each quilt or top have a leeway of about that same amount.

It is important to note that this is not a book promoting the finishing of old tops just for the sake of finishing them, and it is not intended as a bible that tells how one *must* do things. Instead it is a collection of information that I hope will assist those fortunate enough to have old tops. I hope it will help them decide whether or not to quilt them and provide some ways to do so that will give beautiful results.

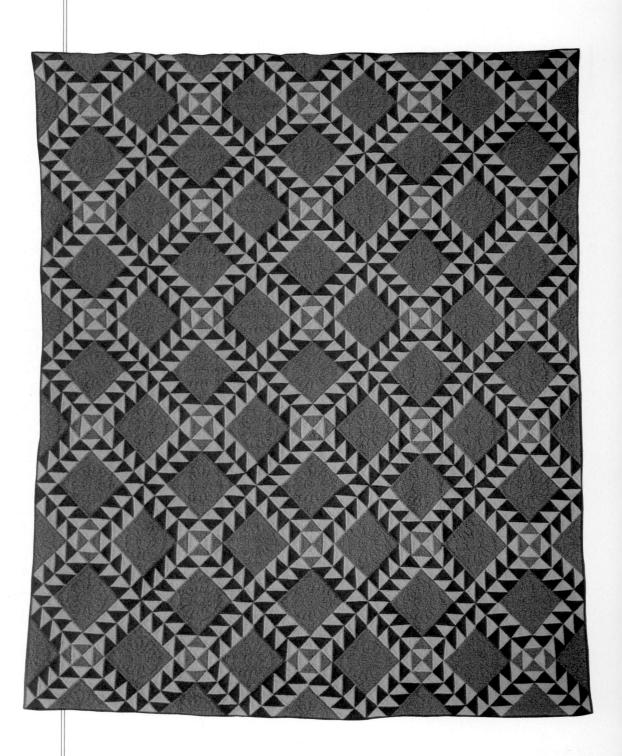

Chapter 1

QUILT TOPS AND TIME-SPAN QUILTS

WHAT IS A TIME-SPAN QUILT?

To understand the meaning of "Time-Span Quilts" we need to know the definitions of "quilt" and "quilt top." Webster defines a quilt as "A bed covering made of two layers of cloth of which the top one is usually pieced or appliquéd and having a filling of wool, cotton, or down held in place by stitched designs or tufts worked through all thicknesses."

The uppermost layer of the quilt is the "top" and is occasionally referred to as the quilt "cover." Though Webster defines the top as usually pieced or appliquéd, many other methods, such as embroidery and stenciling, have been used throughout the years to create a design for the top, including the use of the quilting stitches themselves as the sole design for the quilt. Today painting the fabric, photographic transfers, and other techniques are sometimes used for the top designs.

The backs of quilts are usually plain, made of either a solid or a print fabric. However, some quiltmakers are now making rather elaborate backs for their quilts, something that was quite uncommon until the last few years.

Most quilts are made completely by one individual, but it is not unusual for the top to be made by one person and the quilting to be done by someone else. Sometimes, too, quilts are made by groups. Nevertheless, regardless of who makes them, quilts are generally started and finished within a period of months, or at most a year or two.

Throughout history there have been many tops made and left unfinished, stored away in drawers, trunks, boxes, etc., and many of these are discovered when attics are emptied or estates are closed. When these tops are then found and completed into quilts, the result is a quilt that has been made over a period

Plate 1-1. (left)
LADY OF THE LAKE,
78" x 92", Time span:
c. 1890–1984. Hand pieced,
hand quilted. The top was
made by Mrs. Hatch of
Waterloo, New York, and is
unchanged. It was bound
with a solid green fabric cho-
sen to match the dark green
fabric in the top.

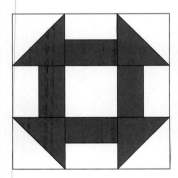

Fig. 1-1. (above)
Simple quilt block.

Plate 1-2. (above)
WHIG ROSE, 86" x 86", c. 1850.
Hand appliquéd, hand pieced. From an estate
in Shelby, Ohio. Incredibly fine workmanship.

Fig. 1-2. (left)
Crazy patch quilt block.

(or time-span) of many years – therefore it is a "Time-Span Quilt." These are the quilts that are the subject of this book.

TYPES AND SOURCES OF QUILT TOPS

Work that quiltmakers have left unfinished over the years ranges from single quilt blocks *(Figure 1-1)* or sets of blocks to partial or completed quilt tops. They are found in all kinds of patterns from a beautiful 1850 WHIG ROSE *(Plate 1-2)* to crazy patches *(Figure 1-2)* assembled with no concern at all for their design. They vary tremendously in condition, from those that are in mint condition to those that are little more than rags.

Until the middle of the 1980's, quilt tops were easily found for very reasonable prices, but today good tops are becoming scarce and may be quite expensive. My collection has come from almost every imaginable source – household, garage, and yard sales, auctions, flea markets, antique shows, classified ads, quilt conferences, thrift stores, gifts from family and friends, and ones passed down in my own family. People settling estates find them in attics, trunks, dresser drawers, or even in places like garages where they may have been used as throws over lumber or autos. One DOUBLE WEDDING RING top I found in a garage sale was covered with paint and had obviously been used as a paint drop cloth.

WHY ARE THERE SO MANY TOPS?

In collecting and handling many quilt tops, it has become evident to me that there are a number of reasons why tops were not completed. Some have been preserved very carefully by their owners either because they were family treasures or merely because they were "lost" in some inaccessible place. Some of the best of these turn up in estate sales. *Plate 1-3* shows a SUNBONNET SUE top that was one of seven identical tops whose maker intended that each of her children and grandchildren someday enjoy a quilt made from her work. Unfortunately, at the estate sale only two of the family members were interested in owning one of the tops.

It is far more common to find tops that are not as well made as the SUNBONNET SUE, are less appealing, or have problems that caused the maker to leave them unfinished. Many kinds of problems are found. For example, some tops will not lie flat. The degree of problems will vary from something major like the overall unevenness of the LONE STAR in *Plate 1-4* to quilts that simply bulge a bit in some places. The LONE STAR top would have to be completely

Plate 1-3. (left)
SUNBONNET SUE,
72" x 85", c. 1935.
*Made by Grace Ainsworth
Wohlers, Rochester, New York.
This is one of seven tops that
were identical except for the
fabric scraps used.*

Plate 1-4. (right)
LONE STAR,
72" x 84", c. 1970.
*Hopelessly out of shape and
made with rather thin fabrics,
this top is an illustration of a
quilt top not worth the time or
effort required to make it into
a quilt.*

Plate 1-5. (above)
FOX AND GEESE, 74" x 88", c. 1895.
Hand and machine pieced. This top was
made by Elizabeth Brower, Fowlerville,
Michigan, and is in mint condition except
that it has no borders.

remade before it would be usable, and
the quality of the fabrics it contains is so
poor that the resulting quilt would hardly
be worth the effort involved.

Another problem often encountered
is that the quilter may have run out of a
fabric and put the work aside until more
could be found. Later, either a suitable
fabric could not be found or the maker
tired of the project. Such a top is shown
in *Plate 1-5* and seems complete except
that it has no borders. Perhaps the quiltmaker ran out of the sashing fabric and
could not find another satisfactory fabric
for making borders.

The lack of borders for some tops
may also have been due to the cost of
fabric. Tops made from scraps required
the purchase of little if any fabric, whereas borders use considerable yardage,
which may have been too expensive for
the quilter to purchase. The top in *Plate
1-6* may be an example of such a situation. Though the center is quite good,
the borders were made from used fabrics
that are thin and stained and quite unac-
ceptable. Maybe it was the only fabric
the quiltmaker could afford, but few
people would want to complete this top
with these borders attached.

One common reason for so many
unfinished tops is that some people preferred piecing to quilting. At one estate

auction I attended, there were about three dozen quilt tops and many boxes of patches (diamonds, triangles, and squares) cut out and ready to be pieced, but only one or two finished quilts. Perhaps the family had already taken all the finished quilts, but to me this seemed to be the estate of a person who definitely enjoyed piecing more than quilting. The TUMBLING BLOCKS top in *Plate 1-7* is one of seven similar tops sold in that auction.

Some people did more piecing than quilting because it was more portable and more easily worked on a few minutes at a time. This allowed a person to carry the project around to different places and/or work on it in spare moments, with the result that tops were sometimes completed rather quickly.

Quilting posed more of a problem. Because quilting frames were large, they were often put on pulleys and raised out of the way when not in use, and floor frames may have been located in less accessible places. This meant that it was not as easy to quilt for short periods of time as it was to piece. As a result, tops accumulated and many were left unquilted.

Other unfinished tops are those that have little or no design, such as squares set together at random with no attempt

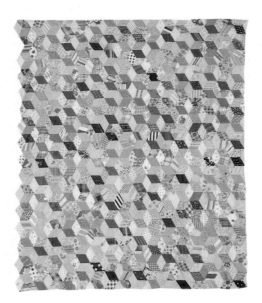

Plate 1-6. (left)
Pattern name unknown, 75" x 75", c. 1940. Borders of worn and faded fabrics having no relationship to the center and quality of the top would have to be removed to make this top appealing and worthy of quilting.

Plate 1-7. (left)
TUMBLING BLOCKS, 76" x 92", c. 1950. Machine pieced. This top was made by Esba M. Malchoff of Sodus, New York. Her estate was auctioned and included about thirty-five other tops and numerous boxes of patches and fabrics.

Plate 1-8. *(above)*
YELLOW STRIP-PIECED,
65" x 88", c. 1940.
Hand and machine pieced.
Though a very appealing
design at first glance, it is
spoiled by the gauzy fabrics
used and the poor workman-
ship. It would be difficult to
make this top into a success-
ful quilt.

to even arrange colors. Similarly, there are tops with poor quality fabrics – thin, raveled, worn, or faded. Though superficially the top in *Plate 1-8* looks interest-ing, it has fabrics that are so sheer they would be difficult to quilt and would not wear well. Some of the seams are already pulling apart.

Tops with little design were probably pieced to use up scraps or to make something that could be tied quickly and used just to provide warmth. Perhaps later there was no need or desire to complete them. The majority of utilitarian tops that I have seen date from the 1930's through the 1960's. They may be good examples of fabrics from those time periods, but most are uninteresting and undesirable to use for making a fin-ished quilt.

Finally, one very probable reason for a top not being completed is that the maker didn't like it after sewing it. Per-haps the colors were a disappointment or the design did not turn out as expect-ed. For example, was the top in *Plate 1-9* actually intended to be a VARIABLE STAR rather than the combination of pinwheels and dark squares that dominate it? It was pieced in units of pinwheels and rectan-gles with squares added in the corners of the blocks *(Figure 1-3)*. If the light and dark values in the rectangles had been reversed, the result would have been a star design *(Figure 1-4)*. Instead, when one looks at the top the stars are visible only upon close examination.

There is really no way of knowing how people felt when they made tops such as these – only that they decided not to quilt them. Doubtless many were set aside because they did not turn out as anticipated and the maker was disap-

Fig. 1-3. *(below)*
Pattern for SARAH'S CHOICE. This drawing shows the units that were sewn for the basic block, as well as the placement of light and dark fabrics as they were actually used in the quilt, top shown in Plate 1-9.

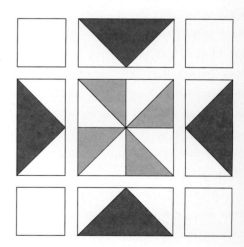

pointed. I'm sure there are many tops being made today that will be set aside for this same reason. (I have already made two!) Years from now, will such tops be discovered and their history questioned just as happens with the old tops we find today?

Plate 1-9. *(right)*
SARAH'S CHOICE, 78" x 78", c. 1940.
Hand and machine pieced. From an estate in Cooper's Plains, New York. The basic block for this top is a VARIABLE STAR with a pinwheel in the center, but because of the placement of the light and dark values, it is difficult to see anything but pinwheels and large dark squares. The placement of lights and darks puts the emphasis on the squares and pin-wheels rather than on the basic VARIABLE STAR block.

Fig. 1-4. *(left)*
By reversing the placement of light and dark fabrics in the rectangular units of each block shown in Fig. 1-3, a star emerges as the dominant design.

Chapter 2

TO FINISH OR NOT TO FINISH

DIFFERING OPINIONS

In a *Quilter's Newsletter Magazine* article published in May 1986, Barbara Brackman wrote about finishing old quilt tops. Another excellent discussion of this topic is a research paper written by Barbara K. Phillippi. In *Uncoverings 1990*, Volume II of the Research Papers of the American Quilt Study Group, Phillippi discusses various opinions about finishing or not finishing pre-1940 quilt tops as expressed by antique dealers, individual owners and collectors, auctioneers, groups that quilt for others, quilt shop owners, and historical society curators throughout western New York State. She also quotes the views of a number of well-known quilt authorities.

Brackman primarily gives the opinions of experts in the quilting field, such as historians, curators, and dealers, whereas Phillippi surveyed a much wider range of people. Although Phillippi found that opinions differed considerably among the professionals she surveyed, among the individuals a large majority felt tops had little value until they were made into finished quilts.

From these studies there is little doubt about how widely opinions vary concerning the finishing of old quilt tops since they obviously differ even among textile conservationists, museum curators, and quilt historians – all people one might expect to be in agreement.

My own opinion on this subject is that the decision about finishing a quilt top must be made individually for each particular top in question. Hopefully the discussions that follow about the pros and cons of finishing tops and what is involved in doing so will help you decide what you want to do with your own quilt top.

Plate 2-1. (left)
PRINCESS FEATHER, 87" x 89", c. 1860. Hand appliquéd, hand assembled, and hemmed. In mint condition. From an estate in Maryland.

NOT TO FINISH

In general, those who favor preserving tops just as they are found point out that there is more historical significance to a top that has not been altered in any way, and it will be more valuable in its original condition. They believe the fabrics in a top can be better examined than fabrics in a quilt because tops can be studied from the back as well as from the front. Moreover, fabrics become fragile or brittle as they age and are apt to be damaged by the handling and needling involved in quilting a top. Some recommend leaving a top unquilted if it is more than fifty or sixty years old, while others believe the fabrics are already showing signs of age in as few as twenty-five years and therefore should not be quilted.

In my work, I have found that most tops that have become brittle were made before 1920. However, there are many earlier tops that are in fine condition. The LADY OF THE LAKE top in *Plate 1-1*, p. 12, was made about 1890, and the fabrics were in mint condition. There were no problems working with it, and the finished quilt is beautiful.

Those who favor preserving tops point out that the selling price of an unquilted top will often be higher than that of a top of equal quality that has been newly finished. Overall, they believe historically, financially, and from the point of view of preservation, old tops should not be quilted.

TO FINISH

The other side of the question is defended by people who favor finishing old tops. Some of them believe a top may actually be better preserved if it is quilted. The edges of the top and the back of the seams are then protected and the top is secured by quilting it to a filler and backing fabric. Some tops have incredibly small seam allowances; others have bias or very stretchy edges, so both factors serve to substantiate this view.

Other people recognize that although the fabrics are not at their best after some undetermined time period and finishing them may be harmful to the fabrics, in the long run, they may actually last longer if they are quilted. The reason for this is that people may take better care of a quilt than a top, thereby prolonging its life. Certainly the kind of use and care a quilt will receive are factors in deciding whether to quilt a top. Quilts made from old tops should receive gentler treatment than new quilts made today with hard use in mind.

Often people want to quilt a top because they feel it was the intent of the original quiltmaker, and the person who made it would like to see the top become a beautiful finished quilt. If the top is one that was passed down in a family, some quilters like the idea of making a two- or three-generation quilt. (An opposite opinion comes from those who think anything done to a top is destroying the integrity of the originator's work, and that the person who made the top would not want someone else to modify it in any way, including quilting it.)

A psychological factor may be involved as well since quilts give so much pleasure to the people who look at or use them. Some of the very people who enjoy a quilt would not enjoy having a top around even as a display piece and would simply store it away in a drawer where it would give pleasure to no one. Some may even look upon a top as useless, thinking it has little, if any, value in an unfinished state. Many of us have heard tales of tops being used as covers for tables, automobiles, pet beds, etc. I found one top covering a display in a flea market and another in that same flea market that was being used to drag a heavy piece of furniture across the floor. There is no question that making a finished quilt from a top will preserve it far better than that kind of use.

A quilter who actually works with an old top, making any needed repairs and completing it with lovely quilting, can get a great deal of satisfaction from the actual process involved and from the additional enjoyment of using the finished quilt. Psychologically the whole process of finishing a top, whether a family heirloom or one of unknown origin, can be very fulfilling.

MAKING A DECISION

These varied opinions may leave you with a sense of turmoil that can only be resolved by deciding for yourself how the historical, financial, and other considerations relate to your own quilt top. Consider what is involved, but once your decision is made, live with it and have no feelings of guilt should others disagree with your opinion. It is your top and should be treated as you wish it to be.

My attitude can best be summarized by looking through this book and studying the examples that follow. Although I do have a few quilt tops that I have not and never will quilt, for the most part I like to see the top turn into something beautiful and useful. Recognizing that Time-Span Quilts are made from older tops, I realize they should be handled more gently than the average quilt made today, and I would not want to see them finished with the intent of using them heavily. But, if we spend months making a beautiful new quilt today, would we not also want to handle it carefully so that it would have a long, useful life? Certainly, too, whenever a top is finished, good workmanship and excellent quilting should be used so that we end up with a beautiful finished quilt.

PRACTICAL CONSIDERATIONS

The opinions noted above are primarily historical and monetary considerations about finishing old quilt tops. There are also some very practical factors that will affect whether you want to finish your particular quilt top.

Probably the most important is the top's condition. Unfortunately, all tops are not in perfect condition, but some could still make lovely quilts if repaired, cleaned, or modified in some way. If the quality of the fabrics is poor, if seams are raveled, if there are stains, or if a large amount of repair work is needed, then you must ask four basic questions to determine whether the top is worth finishing.

Number one: Is it possible to put the top into good condition? (Will the fabric quality hold up to quilting? Can loose seams and other defects be repaired? Can major stains be removed? Was the top made by hand or by machine?)

Number two: How much work will be involved to finish it? (This, of course, is very dependent on decision number one.)

Number three: Does the top have the potential to be a pleasing and/or useful quilt – one that will appeal to you?

Number four: How much does this top mean to you? Some of the above questions will be influenced by sentimental value. If the top has been handed down in your family or if it was given to you by someone special, then you will be willing to put more effort into finishing it than if you acquired it in some other way.

We find, then, that the practical decision about finishing a top depends on four factors: its condition, the work that will be involved, its potential as a finished quilt, and how much completing it means to you. These decisions will be discussed in detail in the following chapters. Examples of tops that I would leave unfinished are discussed and a variety of excellent tops suitable for finishing are shown in the Gallery of Quilt Tops at the end of this chapter.

TOPS TO LEAVE UNFINISHED

Shown in *Plate 2-1,* page 20, is a PRINCESS FEATHER quilt top that I will never quilt. It was made in the mid-

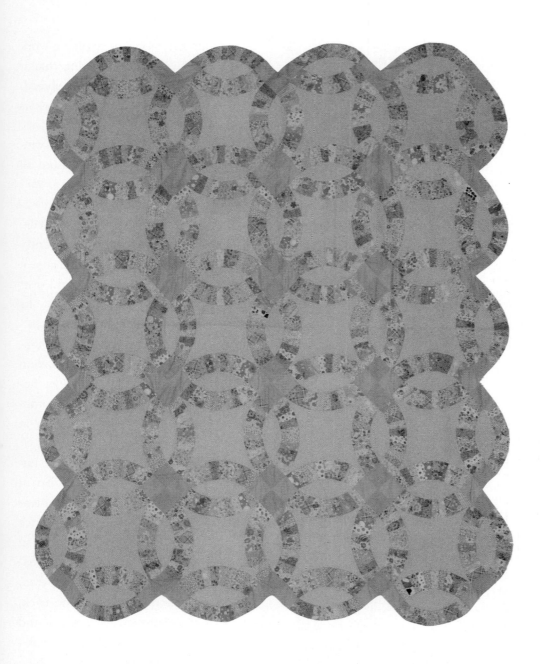

Plate 2-2. *(left)*
DOUBLE WEDDING RING,
71" x 88", c. 1930.
Hand pieced and hemmed by
Mrs. Vernon Croop, Rochester,
New York. Because of the
hemmed edges, it appears this
top was intended for a sum-
mer spread, rather than for
a quilt.

Plate 2-3. (right)
GLITTERING STARS,
65" x 83", c. 1910.
The thin fabrics, stains, and
several tears make this top
unsuitable for quilting, but its
construction is very interest-
ing. Three blocks were hand
pieced and the remainder
were machine appliquéd. The
white fabric pieces were put
on top of red backing squares
and sewn in place by
machine.

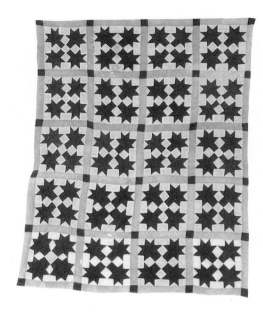

1800's with incredibly fine appliqué work and it was hemmed, indicating that it was probably meant as a summer spread. Because it was appliquéd, the back is smooth, and since the edges are finished, there is no further concern about completing it. Historically, it is a treasure all too rarely seen.

A decision about the top in *Plate 2-2*, page 25, is similar, but more difficult. It, too, was hemmed and apparently never meant to be quilted, but because it is pieced, the seams are rough and over time will tend to ravel or pull out. Its probable use, therefore, should be a factor in deciding whether to leave it unfinished. If used sparingly as a decoration or table cover, it would not require finishing, but as a bed cover it would probably benefit from being quilted – or at least having a back added.

Another quilt top that I will not finish is the GLITTERING STARS top in *Plate 2-3*. This top is stained; it has a tear and some open seams; and the fabrics are thin – all problems that make quilting it seem undesirable to me. The main reason for keeping it unfinished, however, is its construction. Looking at the back, one sees three blocks that are red and white, while the others all appear solid red with white lines of machine stitching showing *(Plate 2-4)*. The two-color

Plate 2-4. (right)
GLITTERING STARS (reverse).
From the back it can be seen
that three blocks were pieced
by hand and the others were
appliquéd by machine.

blocks were pieced by hand using traditional piecing techniques and the other blocks have white patches appliquéd by machine to red backing blocks.

A casual look at this quilt top would not reveal how it was constructed, but as soon as one sees the back it becomes clear. I theorize that the person who made it started to piece the blocks by hand, then decided doing the work by machine would be easier and faster. Since the quality of the machine work is considerably better than that of the hand work, it is obvious that the person was familiar with a machine and used it well. It may, of course, have been completed by a different person.

BRITTLE FABRICS

Some older fabrics become brittle with age, and such old tops I would not knowingly quilt. Quilting would only aggravate the condition, perhaps even causing large tears in the fabrics. An example is the top in *Plate 2-5*. Although the background fabrics in this top seem excellent, several of the prints have small splits indicating deterioration. If such a condition is known, it is certainly unwise to finish the top. On the other hand, if the fabrics are firm and pliable, I would not hesitate to quilt them.

A special note: If you decide to go ahead and quilt your top, don't be intimi-

Plate 2-5. *(above)*
A STRIKING PATTERN, 88" x 90", c. 1880.
Both hand and machine pieced. Though a beautiful top, this one is only suitable for display as a top since the fabrics are quite brittle and would not hold up well to quilting.

dated by people who feel old tops should not be made into quilts. Use your imagination to make it a quilt you will really enjoy and one the maker of the original top would be proud to see. Then take satisfaction in what you have accomplished and enjoy it to the fullest.

USE AND CARE OF QUILT TOPS

If your decision is to not finish your quilt top, it need not be forever stored away. An unfinished top may be displayed in many of the same ways as a quilt: by hanging it on a quilt rack, laying it on the back of a chair, or even hanging it on a wall. Tops can also be hemmed and used as summer spreads or table covers. However, just as a quilt needs care to prevent damage from hanging it and protection from bright light, the same precautions should be taken for a top, and since tops are more fragile than quilts, they need extra protection from hard use or soil.

The least desirable way to care for an old top is to store it away in a drawer or trunk and ignore it for years. If it must be stored, it should be protected from wood, paper, or items that might stain it. A clean, well-rinsed old sheet or pillowcase is good for this purpose. The top should also be refolded occasionally so it does not acquire permanent fold lines.

If you decide you have little interest

in finishing your top or keeping it and it is exceptional or unusual, collectors and museums might be interested in it. Museums specializing in textile collections would take better care of such tops than places that have little knowledge about quilts or textiles, so you might want to do some investigating if you consider such a donation. Remember that compared to the number in existence, relatively few tops will be wanted by museums or collectors. If your top will be considered one of the excess and you still have no desire to finish it, then perhaps you should sell or give it to someone who would appreciate it.

This chapter has clearly shown that before there can be Time-Span Quilts, there must be old quilt tops. They range in quality from spectacular designs in mint condition (rare) to ones with poor fabrics, little planned design, and inferior workmanship. There is usually little, if any, history known about found tops, and one can only guess at their ages and where they were made by using clues from the fabrics or where they were found.

The following gallery of tops gives just a sampling of the wide range of patterns used and the ingenuity of the quilters who designed and sewed them. Most would be appropriate for completion as beautiful Time-Span Quilts.

GALLERY OF QUILT TOPS

Plate 2-6. *(far left)*
DELECTABLE MOUNTAINS,
72" x 82", c. 1880.
Hand pieced by either Anna
Steltz or Rebecca Sheckler of
Bellville, Ohio. Imagine piec-
ing the border on this top.

Plate 2-7. *(left)*
TRIANGLE SQUARES (varia-
tion), 76" x 86", c. 1910.
Hand pieced. From western
New York State. No known
history.

Plate 2-8. *(far left)*
BRICKWORK,
63" x 87", c. 1900.
Hand pieced. From New
Hampshire.

Plate 2-9. *(left)*
SEVEN SISTERS,
68" x 87", c. 1930.
Many fabrics much older
than 1930 are included.
Mostly machine pieced. The
scraps in this top were very
carefully chosen to work well
together.

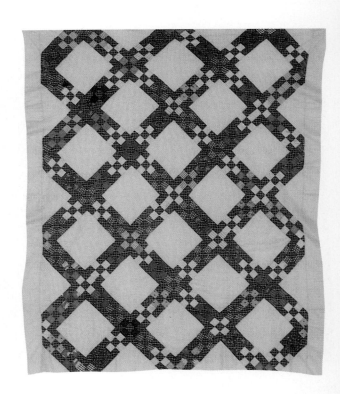

Plate 2-10. *(below)*
ECCENTRIC STAR,
66" x 76", c. 1900.
Hand pieced. From Paducah,
Kentucky.

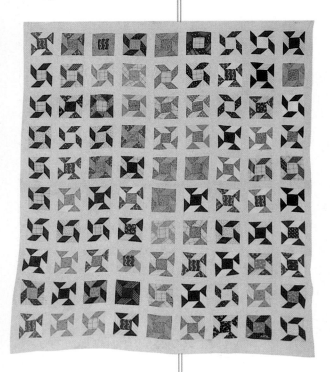

Plate 2-11. *(above)*
NINE-PATCH CHAIN,
73" x 85", c. 1890 and 1920.
Hand pieced. From Ohio.
Though the Nine-Patch blocks
were made before 1900, the
fabric used to complete the
top appears to be a fabric
from the 1920's.

Plate 2-12. *(above)*
PINWHEELS,
74" x 80", c. 1900.
Mostly machine pieced. From
an estate in Maryland.

Plate 2-13. *(below)*
CAESAR'S CROWN,
69" x 90", c. 1940.
Hand and machine pieced.
Rather poor workmanship
detracts from this top, but
the overall effect is quite
attractive.

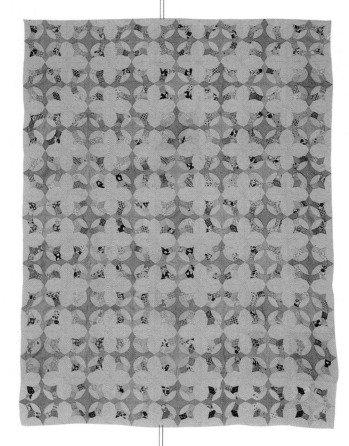

Chapter 3

MAKING REPAIRS

So you have made the decision to finish your quilt top. If it is in mint condition and spotlessly clean, then you won't need this chapter or the next two. Just go ahead: baste it, quilt it, and enjoy it.

Most tops, however, need some work before they can be quilted. This may be repair work, alterations, and/or cleaning. Repair work and alterations should be done *before* any attempt is made to clean a top or remove stains because fibers are subjected to more strain when wet and areas needing repair may be damaged further by washing them. Care should be taken when making repairs to do the work right the first time. If the fabrics are at all fragile, too much reworking can cause more damage than you had initially.

THREAD CHOICE

Quilt tops made before 1950 were made mostly of cotton fabrics, although rayons, silks, and other fabrics are sometimes found – especially in earlier tops. A good rule of thumb is that when making repairs, it is best to use a thread made of the same type of fibers as are in the item being repaired. Therefore, 100 percent cotton thread is the best choice for old tops. Polyester threads did not become readily available for home sewing until after 1960 and are incompatible with the earlier tops.

Another reason to avoiding polyester, cotton-covered polyester, and nylon threads is the fact that they are very strong and might damage the fabrics being repaired. It is generally better to use a thread that is no stronger than the fabric being sewn because it is better to break a thread than to damage the fabric. If, for example, polyester thread were used on a cotton fabric, the cotton might tear before the strong polyester thread would break.

Plate 3-1. (left)
BASKET OF FLOWERS,
73" x 89", c. 1980.
Machine pieced. This is a
copy of a design by Wanda
Dawson of Royal, Nebraska,
which was the Nebraska State
winner in the 1977 Quilts of
America contest sponsored by
Good Housekeeping. *Unfortunately, not all tops are*
found in such fine condition.

LOOSE THREADS

Sometimes even the best tops have loose threads on the back. These should be clipped off carefully with thread snips or scissors and should not be pulled or broken since that could damage a seam or increase raveling.

OPEN SEAMS — REPAIRABLE FABRICS

The most common repairs needed are for open seams. Those may have been caused by poor handling of the top, raveling of the fabrics, seams that weren't well sewn to start with, or seam allowances that were just too tiny to hold together.

The repair needed depends on the circumstances. If the fabrics are firm and the seam allowances are adequate, it is very easy to simply sew the seams back together. Even if the top was pieced by machine, it is usually easier to repair such seams by hand, since it is difficult to sew close to intersections using a sewing machine.

More often than not, however, the seam has pulled apart because one or both of the fabrics have frayed, or because too little fabric was allowed for the seam. If these problems are minor, I have had success placing a piece of seam tape under the seam and stitching it as invisibly as possible to each side of the seam line. This stabilizes the seam without showing from the front of the top. The thread used should match the

Fig. 3-1. (right)
To repair a seam, seam tape is sewn underneath the open seam, using tiny stitches on the upper surface and longer stitches on the seam tape side.

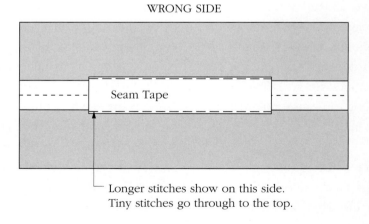

WRONG SIDE

Seam Tape

Longer stitches show on this side.
Tiny stitches go through to the top.

color of the patch in the quilt top and very tiny stitches should be taken on the top of the patch, with slightly longer ones underneath *(Figure 3-1)*. The stitches on top will catch only a couple of threads, but those underneath will be approximately an eighth of an inch long.

If only one of the seam allowances is frayed and the other is firm, the seam tape can first be sewn to the firm seam allowance so that it doesn't show at all, and can then be stitched to the raveled side with the almost invisible stitches just described.

OPEN SEAMS – NONREPAIRABLE FABRICS

All too often the seam is open because the patch has raveled so much it cannot be repaired. Many old tops were made of loosely woven fabrics and not sewn firmly enough to make the seams hold.

Two approaches can be used in such cases. One way is to simply remove the patch and sew in a different one. The second way is to appliqué a new patch over the original one. This second method is the usual procedure when repairing a finished quilt, but with a quilt top, I prefer the first method, which replaces the raveled patch.

In either case, however, the choice of a replacement fabric is very important.

The new patch should be as compatible with the other fabrics in the top as you can possibly manage. This means compatibility for color, type of print, fiber content, and quality. Fabrics from about the same date as those in the top are desirable but are often hard, if not impossible, to find. I see no objection to using more recent fabrics if they look right with the others in the top and have an appropriate fiber content.

Rarely are polyester fabrics or poly-cotton blends a wise choice for such repairs. Polyester fabrics did not come onto the market until the 1950's and 100 percent polyester fabrics look, handle, and wear differently from 100 percent cottons. Poly-cotton blends have similar characteristics, though in some cases the 50/50 blends look more like an all-cotton fabric.

In the last few years textile companies have manufactured fabrics designed as reproductions of some of the old and most familiar designs. They are very useful for making reproductions of old quilts but are less helpful for fabric repairs. Because the fabric and dyes are new, they usually have a different look when placed next to older fabrics in the quilt tops and are therefore easily identified as replacements. *Plates 3-4* and *3-5,* page 37, show some of the reproduction fabrics that are

Plate 3-2. *(left)*
OLD ITALIAN,
74" x 84", Time span: c. 1900–1987.
Hand pieced, hand quilted. The top was from
an antique store in Clarence, New York. The
fabric in the triangles of two blocks was so
badly raveled that it had to be replaced and a
border of new 100 percent cotton fabrics was
added.

Plate 3-3. *(right)*
OLD ITALIAN BLOCK, (detail).
The triangles and center square of this block
were unusable. A new fabric was substituted
that was compatible in color and design with
the other fabrics in the quilt top.

available on the market today.

A good test to decide whether a fabric will look right with the rest of the top is to put a piece of the fabric in the location where it is needed and then look at it from a distance. Color problems or prints that don't seem to be compatible will show up more clearly at a distance. (The effect of distance can also be attained by looking through the wrong end of binoculars or opera glasses.)

The quilt in *Plate 3-2* illustrates these points. It was necessary to replace badly raveled fabrics in two of the blocks. Although the top dates back to around 1900 and the fabrics substituted were no more than ten years old, few people are able to find the new fabrics easily. In each case the patches replaced were the background triangles and center squares. The pink and green block in *Plate 3-3* is particularly difficult to identify as a repaired block. The other block repaired (*Plate 3-2*) is the one with the blue crosses in the upper corner (right side, second row) of the quilt. The original blue fabric in that block seems less compatible with the rest of the top than the new fabric used for the background repair.

TEARS AND HOLES

Often there are one or more holes in a quilt top. Perhaps someone caught the top on something and ripped it; perhaps an animal chewed on it; or maybe one fabric contained a dye that caused deterioration. There are many possible reasons for holes or tears and there are several ways to repair the damage.

If the hole is *very* tiny (less than ¼ inch), I like to fuse a light-weight fusible interfacing underneath the hole. I did this in the quilt in *Plate 3-6*, page 38. Several patches had a print with tiny brown spots in it, and those spots had deteriorated. The holes were no more

Plate 3-4. *(left) REPRODUCTION FABRICS reminiscent of those from the late 1800's. 100 percent cottons.*

Plate 3-5. *(left) REPRODUCTION FABRICS designed to mimic those of the 1930's. 100 percent cottons.*

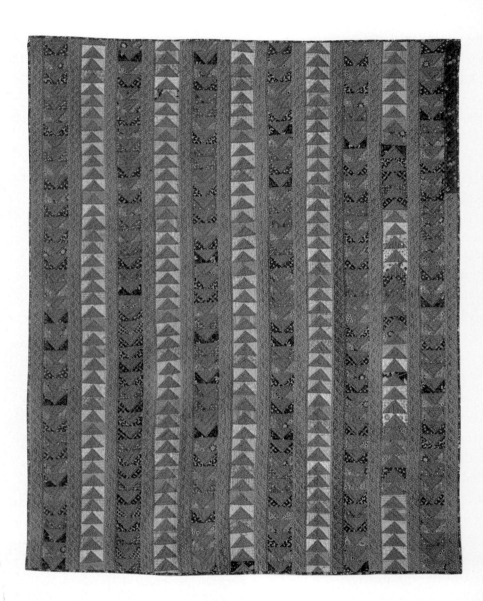

Plate 3-6. *(right)*
FLYING GEESE, 58" x 72",
Time span: c. 1890–1989.
Machine pieced, hand quilt-
ed. The top was from a flea
market in Clarence, New
York. What appear to be
1950's fabrics in two areas
indicate that repairs were
probably made at that time. It
was quilted as found and was
bound with a print fabric.

than an eighth of an inch across, so by using the interfacing method with gray interfacing, the resulting repairs are very difficult to find. *Plate 3-7* shows the back of a block that was repaired in this way.

Usually, however, holes are too large for this method to be appropriate, and in such cases there are at least three ways to repair them. The first is to put a patch underneath the hole and use reverse appliqué to sew the edges of the hole to the patch. The repair fabric underneath should match the color and pattern of the upper fabric in the top as closely as possible. Unless the patch being repaired is quite large, it is better to have the repair fabric fit behind the entire patch. Although this will be a little harder to quilt through, it will minimize any ridge that might show around the hole where the repair patch ends. It is wise to tack the full-size repair patch to the seams around it to hold it in position throughout the repair and quilting process. *Plates 3-8* and *3-9* show the front and back of a patch that has been repaired using this technique.

A second way to repair holes is to cover the whole damaged patch with a new patch and appliqué the new one into position. A third way is to completely replace the damaged patch. In both of these repairs, the same concerns about

Plate 3-7. *(left)*
STAR BLOCK.
The reverse side of this block shows the small piece of fusible interfacing used to repair a tiny hole. Photo by author.

Plate 3-8. *(left)*
Repair of a hole the size of a nickel. Compatible fabric placed behind the hole was reverse appliquéd into place. Photo by author.

Plate 3-9. *(left)*
Reverse side of repair shown in Plate 3-8. The fabric used for the repair covers the entire patch being repaired. Photo by author.

compatibility of fabrics that were discussed under nonrepairable open seams should be considered.

I have heard the suggestion that a hole could be camouflaged by covering it with an appliqué patch. For example, if the top were an appliquéd flower design, it might be possible to add a butterfly or ladybug to cover the hole. In a few cases this might be appropriate, but for most tops, especially those that are pieced, appliqués would usually seem incompatible with the original design.

SHADOWING

Many old tops were made of muslins or other light-colored fabrics that were relatively thin so that dark-colored threads or fabric and dark seam allowances show through the light areas of the top. This is called shadowing. Often such threads and seams are not noticed until the quilt top has been basted and quilting is in progress. At that time it can be very frustrating to discover the shadowing.

Clipping and removing loose threads so they will not shadow is easy and essential. The same is true for the tails that result at the intersections of seams that include pieced triangles. Clipping tails not only prevents shadowing but also reduces bulk at the intersections.

It may, however, be impossible to

Fig. 3-2. (right)
When dark and light patches are sewn together, if the dark seam allowance is wider than the light and they are pressed toward the light patch, a dark line may show (or "shadow through") on the right side of the patch.

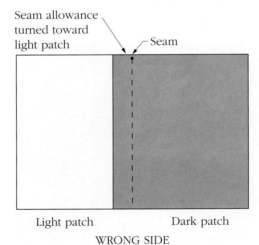

Seam allowance turned toward light patch — Seam

Light patch   Dark patch
WRONG SIDE

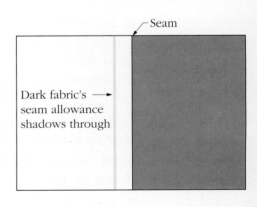

— Seam

Dark fabric's → seam allowance shadows through

RIGHT SIDE

prevent shadowing caused by seam allowances. That problem occurs when a seam allowance is pressed toward a light-colored patch and the dark fabric in the allowance is wider than the light fabric. The dark one then shadows through to the right side. *Figure 3-2* illustrates shadowing.

An obvious way to prevent the seam from shadowing is to press it toward the darker patch, but frequently this cannot be done. A second way is to trim the dark fabric so it is a thread or two narrower than the light fabric, but this too may be impossible if the old top had such narrow seams that any trimming might cause them to pull apart. Therefore, when neither pressing nor trimming seams can be used to prevent shadowing, one must simply accept it. Luckily, shadowing is something that is mostly seen when the quilt is examined closely and does not show with casual viewing. Also, if outline quilting is the quilt design being used, it rather effectively disguises much of the shadowing of seams.

It is wise to examine each top carefully to see if shadowing will occur and decide whether it can be prevented. Please, though, be careful using scissors around any old top. A slip can be disastrous, and a little shadowing is far more acceptable than a hole.

TOPS THAT DON'T LIE FLAT

Often tops are found that do not lie flat because of edges that ripple, patches that are gathered in, tucks, puckering, or similar problems. Sometimes these tops are hopeless – short of taking the entire top apart and starting over again. The LONE STAR top in *Plate 1-4*, page 15, is an example of one that is hopelessly out of shape, but in most cases, the problems can be solved.

A few of these tops, especially those that were hand pieced, will flatten out when they are pressed. Therefore, it is wise to press a questionable top before deciding that there really is a problem.

QUILTING IN

Made without the precise templates and tools that we have today, some of the patches in the old quilts did not fit perfectly and quiltmakers often eased in seams causing some fullness in the block or top. Such minor fullness can usually be *quilted in*, a term that means a small amount of fullness will disappear during the quilting process. The fullness disappears because the batting pads the patches just enough to make the overall quilt seem flat. The more quilting done and the thicker the batting used, the more the fullness can be quilted in.

Though I never want to encourage

inferior work, it is nevertheless a relief to know that in order to get a lovely finished quilt, a top does not have to lie as perfectly flat as we try to make our quilt tops today. Small amounts of fullness will disappear during the quilting process and the quilts in *Plate 8-8*, page 92, *Plate 9-2*, page 99, and *Plate G-1*, page 119 all illustrate this point. None lay completely flat as tops, but all responded well to being quilted in.

INACCURATE SEAMS

A simple problem to solve is a seam that was not properly planned or was sewn wrong. The top of the quilt shown in *Plate 3-10* has seams in the center that cross at right angles, but when they were originally sewn, the angle was incorrect. There was excess fabric in the seams, making the top bulge badly in the middle. By opening the seams and sewing them again at the correct angle, the top

Plate 3-10. *(right)*
PINK MEDALLION, *(detail).*
Center area of quilt shown in Plate 4-8, page 55. Incorrectly sewn seams made the center bulge, but when taken apart, the seams were easily re-sewn at right angles to make the center lie flat.

Plate 3-11. *(far right)*
LOG CABIN STRAIGHT FURROWS, *(detail).*
Quilt top in Plate 3-12 folded to the back. The blocks on the outer rows of this top were larger than those in the center, making the edges 4 to 5 inches longer than the center area. Photo by author.

was flattened out. On the other hand, if too little fabric has been used in a seam, there is probably no solution short of taking the top completely apart and re-cutting all of the pieces.

The top for the quilt in *Plate 3-12* was another that did not lie flat. It was longer on both sides than in the middle and looked very much out of shape. No attempt to flatten it worked. I finally real-ized the problem was caused because the blocks in the outer rows were larger than those in the middle rows. This can be seen in *Plate 3-11*, which shows the blocks along the edge that is folded over are larger than those in the middle of the top. The outer blocks each measured 6 inches and the inner blocks were 5½ inches. I decided to move two rows of the large blocks from one side of the top to the other side. It worked, and although the finished quilt is not a true rectangle (one side is 80 inches long and

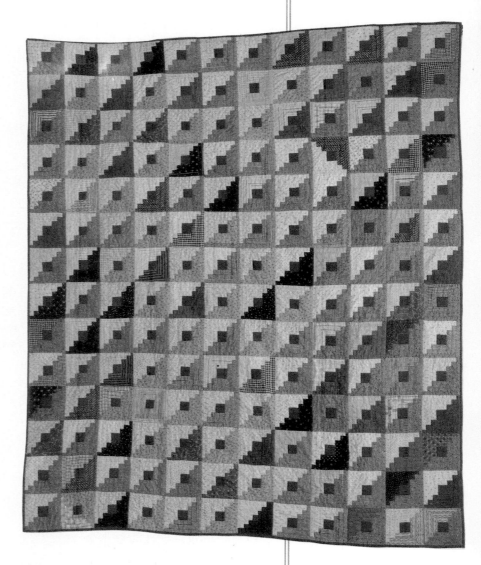

Plate 3-12. *(right)*
LOG CABIN STRAIGHT FURROWS,
70" x 82", Time span: c. 1900–1989.
Hand pieced on backing squares, machine quilted in the ditch. The top was from a Clarence, New York, flea market. It was modified to make it lie flat and was bound in red to match the red in the center squares of each block.

the other is 84 inches), that is not obvious and the quilt now lies flat.

TIGHTLY STITCHED SEAMS

The two quilts just mentioned bring up still another problem that affects many repairs – seams that are too small or too tight to be opened without damaging the fabric. The LOG CABIN *(Plate 3-12,* page 43 and *Plate 3-11,* page 42) was sewn by hand, so the seams were easily taken apart. The PINK MEDALLION *(Plate 3-10,* page 42) was pieced by machine, but the stitches were long enough that they did not cause a problem. In many cases, however, the maker used machine stitches so small it is impossible to take them apart without damaging the fabric. I have found this to be particularly true of older tops, especially those made before 1900, and it makes me wonder if people just beginning to use sewing machines felt they had to use very small stitches to assure

Plate 3-13. (right)
BASKET QUILT, (detail).
Quilt top in Plate 3-14.
Shown in this block is an
example of the problems
found throughout this top
caused by inaccurate piecing.
The fullness was adjusted
during the quilting process by
taking tucks and quilting in.
Photo by author.

sturdy seams.

Solving a problem for patches sewn with such tiny stitches can be done, though not by what many would call good quiltmaking techniques. I had an old top passed down in our family that at first seemed impossible to finish because there was so much excess fullness in many blocks. It was made from thin red and blue fabrics that I think must have been old flag bunting. Those were combined with a very tightly woven muslin. Most of the top was sewn by machine using about 30 stitches to the inch, so any attempt to take apart a seam was hopeless without damaging those thin, colored fabrics.

Since this top had sentimental value and the potential to be nice if completed, I barged ahead, basting it and trusting that I could solve the problems while quilting it. *Plate 3-13* shows two of the blocks as they appeared after the top had been basted but not yet quilted. What I did was make tucks and blindstitch them down to flatten each block as I quilted. The careful choice of a quilting pattern that did not require stitching through the tucks was very important since there were too many layers of very tough fabric to allow any quilting through them. The end result, shown in *Plate 3-14,* was to me pleasing and definitely worth the effort. Though the blocks are not square and the quilt would not be considered excellent by any standards, it is still a quilt that I am glad I completed.

Usually fullness within blocks that is too much to quilt in doesn't require such drastic action as taking tucks but can be dealt with merely by loosening a seam, adjusting the fabrics, and blindstitching them back together. I usually do this while I am quilting. The quilt sandwich has been basted, so the top and back lie straight against each other. (Basting should be quite close together in such cases.) When I put the quilt into a hoop, it is easy to see just how much fullness there is in a particular patch. I release the seam, make the adjustment, and re-sew the seam with a blindstitch. This could be done before the top is basted if placed on a flat, firm surface while making the adjustments, but sometimes it is easier to see what is needed during the quilting process than before the top has been basted.

RIPPLED EDGES

Still another problem frequently encountered is edges that ripple. This problem is common in old tops and is usually caused by borders that are longer than the central area of the top. In many

Plate 3-14. *(above)*
BASKET QUILT, 74" x 79",
Time span: c. 1870–1986. Hand and machine pieced, hand quilted. The top was made by Lila Land Chun of Bartow, Georgia, shortly after the Civil War and was handed down through the family of the author. Minimal quilting was done because of problems with the workmanship of the top and the fabrics used.

of these tops, the center area was pieced by hand, but the borders were added by machine. Therefore, if the center was stretched while the border was added, the result was a border that rippled. The top in *Plate 3-15* is a good example. The stars are hand pieced and were obviously stretched too much as the borders were added by machine. Such a problem can be solved easily by removing the border, cutting it to the correct size, and re-sewing it to the top.

With tops that have no borders, rippling usually occurs because the edges have been stretched, a problem most commonly seen when the patches along the edges have been cut on the bias. Pressing each patch with the straight grain of the fabric may solve the problem – or at least improve it *(Figure 3-3)*. For

tops that ripple along the edges even after careful pressing, it may be necessary to gather the edges slightly. To do this, a gathering thread is sewn all around the edge of the top. I prefer to gather by hand using stitches that are between ⅛ and ¼ inches long. Using a machine is less desirable since it may cause additional stretching of the edges, but if you chose to work by machine, it may help to use an even feed (or walking) foot. The machine stitch length should be about six stitches to the inch.

After sewing the gathering thread, the top is placed on a flat surface and the thread is drawn up just enough so the edge can be flattened. Any fullness that results within the patches will usually quilt in easily.

Once flat, a row of staystitching will stabilize the edges, keeping them flat while the top is being quilted. The staystitching can be sewn at the same time the quilt is being basted and can be done whether the quilt is basted in a basting frame or on a large flat surface. The top, batting, and back are layered, being careful to keep the tension equal between them. Then at each edge small staystitches are sewn through all three layers, checking and adjusting the gathering threads a bit more if needed to be sure the edge of the top lies flat with the other layers.

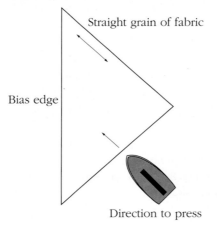

Straight grain of fabric

Bias edge

Direction to press

Fig. 3-3. *(right)*
Press with the straight grain of the fabric to help smooth a bias edge.

Plate 3-15. *(left)*
BLAZING STARS,
62" x 84", c. 1880–1920.
The hand-pieced stars were
assembled by machine. The
eight-sided pattern of the stars
and the fabrics within them
suggest that they were made
around 1880. The fabrics
used to set them together are
more typical of the 1920's,
indicating that the stars were
pieced earlier and assembled
at a later date.

Chapter 4

ALTERATIONS

SHOULD QUILT TOPS BE ALTERED?

Up to this point, the repairs discussed have involved only minor changes in a quilt top. There are, however, many tops that are incomplete, sets of blocks that could be made into a top, or tops that have little design value. How much one should do about completing or changing such items is a matter of controversy.

I was once asked whether I felt I was violating the intent of the original quiltmaker and the integrity of the top by changing something. I think the person who started it would be delighted to have an unfinished top completed and/or an uninspiring design improved. I like to think that all quiltmakers, past and present, want something beautiful to result from their efforts. If by altering the original top I can make a plain top attractive, complete a partial top, or make a set of blocks become a beautiful

finished quilt, then I feel the originator would approve of my efforts.

Of course, my opinion differs from people today who want to save everything just as it is found. It is therefore something that must be thought out and decided by the individual who owns the blocks or top in question.

There is still another factor that influences this decision and that is the amount of work involved if one decides to change a top.

An interesting example of both of these points can be seen in the SISTER'S CHOICE top in *Plate 4-2,* page 50. The traditional placement of patches *(Figure 4-1,* page 50)* is seen only in a few of the blocks. In others, the patches were turned in many different ways so at first glance it is hard to see just what block pattern was used. To make the blocks conform to the usual Sister's Choice pattern would require taking the top almost

Plate 4-1. *(left)*
*FLYING GEESE, 57" x 80",
Time span: c. 1870–1986.
Hand pieced and hand quilted. The top came from a church antique show. It was quilted without any changes and was bound in a solid red fabric.*

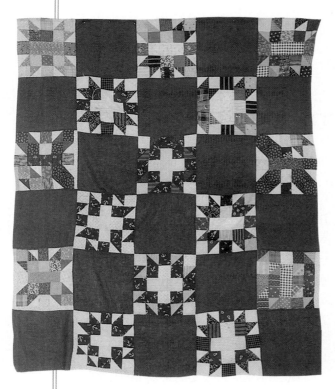

Plate 4-2. *(above)*
SISTER'S CHOICE, 58" x 68", c. 1900.
Hand pieced. This is an interesting top to
study because of the haphazard way the
patches were combined. Many were turned so
the Sister's Choice design is not recognizable.
Was this intentional or accidental?

Fig. 4-1. *(left)*
Traditional Sister's Choice quilt block. Those
in Plate 4-2 vary widely, and even when they
follow the traditional placement for patches,
they do not include the dark center square.

completely apart and would involve a great deal of work. One can also wonder if perhaps the original quiltmaker made it this way deliberately and enjoyed the variety of the many different blocks. Is it then a top that you would want to redo or is it one you can enjoy just for the fun of it?

FABRICS FOR ALTERATIONS

If additions or changes are going to be made in a top, the fabrics used should be compatible with the original in both color and design. If fabrics of the same vintage as those in the top can be found, that is ideal, but it is usually impossible to find such fabrics in sufficient yardages to use for big projects such as borders. Naturally, if found, the search can be very rewarding.

One of the best places to look for vintage fabrics is with vendors at quilt conferences. Some of them specialize in old quilts and tops and frequently have older fabrics for sale. Shops that handle antique quilts sometimes handle vintage fabrics as well, and such finds sometimes turn up in antique shops, flea markets, household or garage sales, and even auctions.

Because it is quite unusual to find an antique fabric that seems ideal, or even adequate, for a given remodeling project, one is therefore dependent on finding new fabrics that look appropriate with the top. The search can be very frustrating and may take months or even years, but it is most rewarding when just the right fabric is finally found.

Sometimes compatible fabrics simply cannot be found. This was the case for the top seen in the FLYING GEESE quilt in *Plate 4-1,* page 48. The top was not made in a block format, but I felt it would benefit from a border similar to the long strips that separated the rows of flying geese. After four years I realized I was searching in vain and solved the problem by just using a red binding. There is enough red in the quilt that the color is appropriate. Also, red is a powerful color and although the binding is narrow, it is bright enough to serve as a frame for the quilt. The new solid-colored fabric matched many of the small red triangles in the quilt and hence looked right.

Another choice can occasionally be made as it was in the STYLIZED FLOWERS quilt in *Plate 4-3.* The top was made in the thirties and the green used for the leaves (often called Depression green) is quite different from the greens on the market today. In this case, the right color for a binding was a fabric from a series of specially dyed fabrics being sold today in quilt shops and at many quilt conferences.

BORDERS

One of the most frequent alterations that may be considered for an old top is the addition of borders. I find that I like borders on most old and new quilts. Just as an artist frames a painting, a well planned and appropriate border can add a frame to a quilt and serve as a lovely finishing touch.

Needless to say, this is not true in every situation, and with old tops a border should definitely not be added if it will not be compatible with the original top. It would be wrong to add a border just because some quilt authority said all quilts should have borders or because the top is small and a wide border would make it more usable.

Tops made in a block and lattice for-

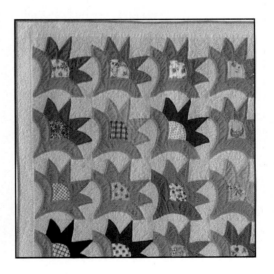

Plate. 4-3. (left)
STYLIZED FLOWERS, detail of quilt in Plate 8-10, page 95. To find an appropriate color for the binding of this quilt, it was necessary to use a fabric dyed to match the green in the leaves.

mat almost always seem unfinished if they have no borders because the individual blocks appear to be falling off the edge of the quilt. This may be one reason why many old tops were unfinished. The maker ran out of the lattice fabric and could not find more of the same fabric or something similar that would go with the rest of the top.

The FOX AND GEESE top in *Plate 1-5,* page 16, illustrates this point. It is a beautiful top with excellent workmanship, but the fabric used for the sashing is an unusual shade of lavender. I bought the top at an auction in 1986, and watched for a compatible fabric for years with little success. Though I have one fabric that could have been used, the color is close rather than exact, and the design is a tiny check that is different from any of the prints in the top. Rather than use something that was almost right,

I preferred to enjoy the top as a top until just the right fabric came along. Finally, about two years ago, I was rewarded for waiting when a reproduction fabric came onto the market that was an exact match.

Another border example is the OLD ITALIAN quilt in *Plate 3-2,* page 36. The top had no borders and seemed to need them. Luck was with me because I walked into a fabric store and quickly found a gray, 100 percent cotton, homespun fabric in a closely matching color and pattern. I could hardly believe my luck. But the red squares to go with the ones in the top proved to be a real problem. It is an unusual red and it took over two years before I found something I felt was appropriate in both color and design. (My supply of red homespun fabrics grew noticeably during that period since I purchased many quarter-yard pieces to try with the top.) The wait was well worthwhile, however, because it resulted in a finished border that fits well with the sashing in the top.

Using a binding as a substitute for a border works in many cases. This was done for the FLYING GEESE quilt in *Plate 4-1,* page 48, and for the LOG CABIN quilt in *Plate 3-12,* page 43, and for the TRIANGLES AND DIAMONDS quilt in *Plate 9-2,* page 99. In each case a color was chosen that was dominant in

Plate 4-4. (right)
HANDS ALL AROUND,
85" x 85", (Center: 60" x 60").
Hand and machine pieced.
Found in Paducah, Kentucky. The white border of this top not only totally overpowers the design of the center but is poorly attached with a great deal of fullness. It is a good example of why borders should not be added just to make a top a larger size.
Photo by author.

the top and was a dark or strong color. As borders these same strong colors would have overpowered the center of the quilts, but as bindings they worked very well to frame them.

Adding a wide border merely to increase the size of the top is usually inappropriate. Wide borders often overpower the central section of a quilt and seem out of proportion to the overall design. This is seen in the top shown in *Plate 4-4*, page 52, where the very wide borders do not coordinate at all well with the pieced center of the top.

Another, and frequently better, answer might be to complete the top as a small throw or lap quilt rather than changing its design by adding borders. Or, if you want to finish the top and do want it to be larger, you could consider multiple borders coordinated so they fit into the design of the original top. The NINE-PATCH quilt in *Plate 5-5*, page 61, shows a good use of repeat borders to make the quilt the desired size.

SASHES

The TULIP quilt in *Plate 4-5* presented a different problem. The tulips were appliquéd onto large blocks and appeared to be too far apart, but the most noticeable problem was the fabric used for the background and the fact that

Plate 4-5. *(above)*
TULIPS, 63" x 87", Time span: c. 1950–1992. Hand appliquéd, machine quilted. The top came from an auction in Bergen, New York, and is made from linen-type fabrics too heavy for hand quilting. The narrow lavender sashing and binding were added and are made of a fabric from the same era as the top.

Plate 4-6. (right)
SWING IN THE CENTER,
73" x 86", c. 1920.
Hand pieced. Found in a
Paducah, Kentucky, antique
store. The missing upper block
could be replaced with either
a matching pink vintage fab-
ric or a new fabric dyed to
match. It would be so difficult
to match the fabric for a
pieced corner block that
muslin might be used to
provide a plain area for a
signature block or a special
quilting design.

Plate 4-7. (far right)
NINE-PATCH, 60" x 78",
Time span: c. 1900–1993.
Hand pieced, hand quilted.
The top came from Georgia.
Blocks varied in size resulting
in rows that were different
lengths. These were evened
out and borders were added.

the blocks, when assembled, left visible seam lines that were crooked and distracting. Because the background fabric was very coarse and heavy, and the blocks had been assembled with tiny machine stitches, it was impractical to take them apart to re-sew them. The answer was to add narrow sashing between the tulips, thereby covering the crooked lines and framing the individual blocks. The fabric chosen was from about 1950 and seemed compatible with the appliquéd tulips.

INCOMPLETE TOPS

All too often we find tops that are missing a section as seen in *Plate 4-6.* They may have great potential, which makes us want to complete them, but again the problem arises of trying to find fabrics that are compatible with the original. For a top like this one, finding a pink fabric to complete the corner is not too difficult, particularly since today fabric dyeing has become so common. Since it would be difficult or nearly impossible to make another pieced block that would match the originals, I would either use the pink for the entire missing area or use it for one block and a muslin for the corner. If muslin were used, it would make an ideal place to put the history of

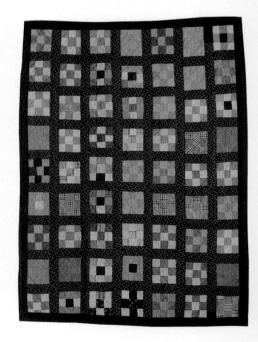

the top and the signature of the person who completed the quilt.

Rarely is one so lucky as I was for the CHURN DASH quilt shown in *Plate 5-7,* page 62. I bought the top at an auction in a box with several other old tops. Though I knew it had borders on only three sides, I also knew there were some strips of the red fabric in the bottom of the box. Luckily, those turned out to be enough to make the fourth border and complete the top without having to add any new fabric.

Usually, however, matching fabrics are not available. The red NINE-PATCH top used to make the quilt shown in *Plate 4-7* had no borders and the sashing in several places was not complete. A red print fabric from the late 1980's seemed compatible in both color and print design, so I used it to complete the sashes and make a border for the top.

MAJOR CHANGES

The PINK MEDALLION and green NINE-PATCH quilts shown in *Plates 4-8* and *4-9* are examples made from quilt tops I felt required major changes before they were worth quilting. When found, the pink top was being used as a cover for a booth at a flea market. The center did not lie flat. A thin print fabric was used in each corner that was totally dif-

ferent from the colors or quality of the rest of the top, and two corners even had holes in them. In the photo of this quilt *(Plate 4-8),* one piece of this fabric was pinned in place to show how the corners of the top looked when found. By removing the print fabric and making new corners of fabrics similar to those in the original top, the result had colors and a design that seemed coordinated and appealing. The outer blue border was also added.

Plate 4-8. *(above) PINK MEDALLION, 68" x 80", Time span: c. 1920–1987. Machine pieced, hand quilted. The top was found covering a booth in a flea market in Clarence, New York. Originally the corners were all made from the print fabric pinned in one corner in the photo. These corner areas were replaced and the border added. A solid pink fabric was used for the backing and binding.*

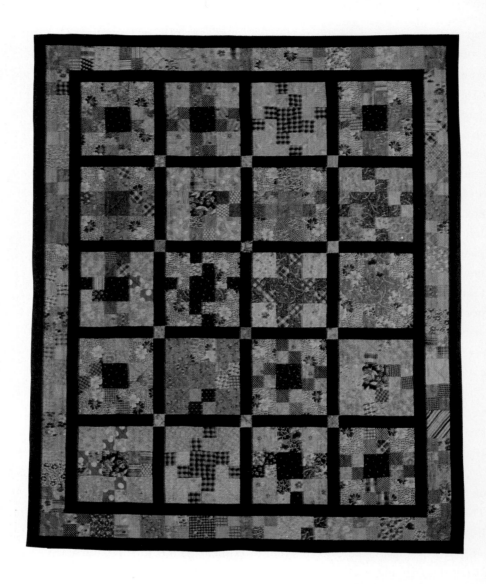

Plate 4-9. *(right)*
NINE-PATCH,
65" x 78", Time span:
c. 1940–1988. After alter-
ations. Machine and hand
pieced, machine quilted. The
top, from Atlanta, Georgia,
was separated into Nine-
Patch blocks and sashing
strips. New fabric from the
1950's was used for the sash-
ing and dark borders. The
original sashing strips were
used for the pieced border. It
was quilted with nylon thread
in an overall grid design.

The NINE-PATCH quilt *(Plate 4-9)* was even more of a challenge. The original top had patches that blended together into a hodgepodge of squares and Four-Patches *(Plate 4-10)*. Upon examination, I realized it was really pieced as Nine-Patch blocks and assembled with sashing made of plain and pieced squares similar to the patches in the Nine-Patch blocks *(Figure 4-2)*. Since the print fabrics used in both the blocks and sashes were similar, the design did not show at all.

Remodeling involved taking the top apart to give twenty Nine-Patch blocks plus strips of sashing and then using a new dark green fabric to make new sashes. The dark fabric set off the 1930's fabrics of the original top and ended the confusion caused by blocks and sashing that were too similar. I made the border by using the original sashing framed by more of the new dark green fabric. Though not a prizewinner, it is far more interesting than the original and makes a pleasing utilitarian quilt.

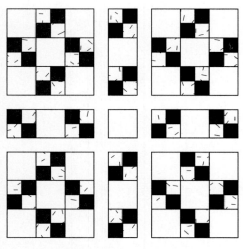

Nine-Patch Block   Sashing   Nine-Patch Block

Plate 4-10. *(far left) NINE-PATCH, before alterations. Shown here is about half of the top as it was found. Initially, it appeared to a jumble of Four-Patch and plain squares. Close examinations showed that it was actually constructed as Nine-Patches and sashings. (See Figure 4-2.) Photo by author.*

Fig. 4-2. *(left) This diagram shows how the original top combined Nine-Patch blocks and pieced sashing.*

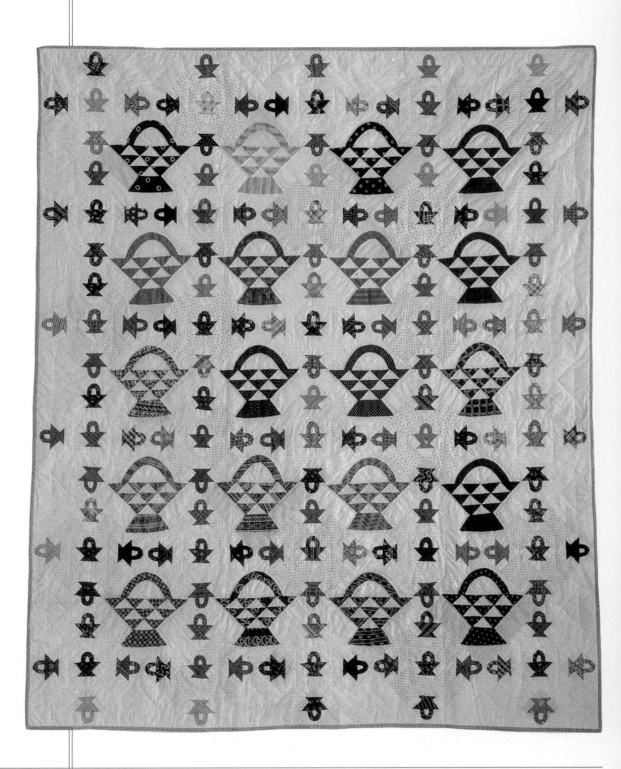

Chapter 5

QUILTS FROM BLOCKS AND PARTS

BLOCKS

Just as quilt tops are searched for, so too are single quilt blocks and groups of blocks. Single, one-of-a-kind blocks are especially popular for block collections, and individual blocks that seem to go together work well for sampler quilts, such as the one shown in *Plate 5-2,* page 60. When fortunate enough to find a set of matching blocks, they can often be made into beautiful quilts, as illustrated by the BLUEBIRDS quilt in *Plate 5-3,* page 61. The embroidered squares used for this quilt were found as a set.

When it comes to the repair and cleaning of blocks, the same guidelines apply that apply to tops. (See Chapter 6 for information about cleaning.) Fortunately, blocks have usually been packed away so that they are rarely soiled or in need of repair.

Many considerations come into play when planning to make quilt blocks into a quilt or wallhanging. The number of blocks will influence the size of the finished product and the way the blocks can be successfully combined. The type of block will affect their set – whether they should be combined with or without sashing or with alternate plain blocks. Any fabrics added for finishing the blocks should be carefully chosen for compatibility of color and design. Some of these considerations are illustrated by the following examples:

The quilt in *Plate 5-1* was made from two sets of basket blocks, both made by the same person. By using the small blocks as cornerstones between the lattices, the two sizes were combined to make an outstanding quilt. Fabric for the lattices was found with the blocks and used in their construction.

In the PIECED FLOWERS quilt in *Plate 5-4,* page 61, there were only nine blocks available. When spread out it was

Plate 5-1. *(left)*
HIDDEN SECRETS, 65" x 79", Time span: c. 1890–1993. Hand pieced and hand quilted. Basket blocks in two sizes were pieced by Phoebie Ogilsbie between 1880 and 1890. The top was assembled using yardage found with the blocks and quilted by Clara Pope of Syracuse, New York. Clara chose the name for this quilt because one of the small basket blocks had a man's name written on the back.

Plate 5-2. *(above)*
SAMPLER, 42" x 55",
Time span: c. 1900–1988.
Hand pieced and hand quilt-
ed. The blocks for this sampler
were handed down in her
family and were assembled
and quilted by Ruth Norton,
Rochester, New York.

obvious that they were best combined without sashing since a very interesting secondary pattern unfolded at the corners where the blocks came together. This meant only a small quilt could be made unless wide borders were added, and since that seemed inappropriate, making a small quilt became the better answer. Though borders were added, they are in proportion to the rest of the top. The 100 percent cotton fabric used for the border is more loosely woven than the typical cottons used in quilts today, but it was chosen because of its compatibility with the blocks in both color and design. I did the quilting with

an outline stitch on the flowers and a grid in the background – quilting designs that might have been used at the time the blocks were made.

The BLUEBIRDS quilt in *Plate 5-3* would likewise have been quite small if the blocks had been pieced together side by side, but in this case it seemed appropriate to make them into a larger top. Blue sashing and borders not only increased the size but also highlighted the blue embroidery.

Again there were not enough blocks available for the NINE-PATCH quilt in *Plate 5-5* to make a full-sized quilt using the blocks alone. Since Nine-Patch blocks show up best when separated, alternate plain blocks served both that purpose and to provide additional size. A dark fabric was chosen to enhance the Nine-Patch blocks and a diagonal set was used to add interest. A series of borders both framed the center and helped to enlarge the top to the desired size.

A second problem existed with these blocks because they varied somewhat in size. Although the ones used in the center varied by as much as a half inch, they were close enough that they could be trimmed to a common size without being obvious. But the four at the corners of the borders were too large to be used with the others. By making the width of

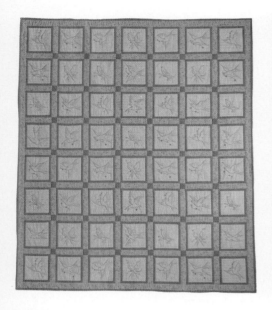

Plate 5-5. *(left)*
*NINE-PATCH, 78" x 96",
Time span: c. 1930–1987.
Hand and machine pieced,
machine quilted. The blocks
were a gift from a friend and
included some from two time
periods. Dark fabrics and
triple borders were used to
give the quilt an Amish look.
Nylon thread was used for the
quilting.*

Plate 5-3. *(above)*
*BLUEBIRDS,
76" x 87", Time span: c. 1920–1992.
Hand embroidered, machine assembled and
quilted. The blocks for this quilt were found in
Rochester, New York. The blue sashing and
borders were added to complement the
embroidered blocks.*

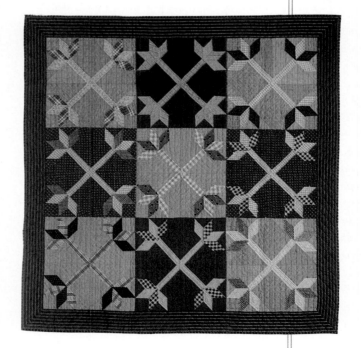

Plate 5-4. *(right)*
*PIECED FLOWERS,
58" x 58", Time span: c. 1910–1991.
Hand pieced, hand quilted. The blocks were
from Atlanta, Georgia. Two small holes near
the edges were repaired and the border and
back were made from a fabric of unknown
vintage.*

Plate 5-6. (right)
CHURN DASH, 48" x 56",
Time span: c. 1890–1992.
Hand pieced and quilted. The
blocks were made by the
mother of Catherine Schantz
of Rochester, New York. They
were assembled and quilted
and are owned by Ruth Norton of Rochester, New York.
Compare this quilt in which
the pieced blocks are set side
by side to the quilt in Plate 5-
7 where the blocks are separated from each other by
unpieced squares.

Plate 5-7. (far right)
CHURN DASH, 79" x 99",
Time span: c. 1930–1991.
Machine pieced and hand
quilted. The top was from an
estate auction in Coopers
Plains, New York. Because the
pieced blocks were assembled
with alternate plain blocks
between them, the appear-
ance is quite different from
the Churn Dash quilt in
Plate 5-6.

the borders the same width as the patches in these corner blocks, the size difference from the blocks in the center of the
top is not obvious. Quilting was done by
machine in an overall grid pattern with
monofilament nylon thread (see Chapter
8) so it would blend with both the light
fabrics in the blocks and the dark background color.

When working with blocks, one
should consider both the size of the quilt
that can be made from them and the
effect created when they are placed side
by side compared to that achieved when
the blocks are separated. The comparison of these two sets is shown well by
the quilts in *Plate 5-6* and *Plate 5-7*. Both
are Churn Dash patterns, but the results
are very different.

The larger quilt (*Plate 5-7*) has only
31 Churn Dash blocks, whereas the
smaller one has 56 (*Plate 5-6*), but
because alternate plain squares were
used in the red one, the result was a
much larger quilt. Also, there is a totally
different appearance created by the secondary designs that occur in the quilt
where the blocks are set side by side
compared to the one in which the blocks
are separated.

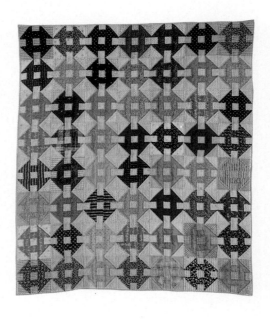

PARTS

It is not uncommon to find quilt tops that were started and never completed. With a little imagination these can often be used to make delightful quilts.

The quilt in *Plate 5-8* was made from an incomplete top. When found, it was four blocks wide and eight blocks long, which is definitely not a usual size for a quilt. In addition, two blocks were damaged. By the removal of two rows of blocks at the ends, elimination of the two damaged blocks, and use of the remaining blocks to add a row along one side, the resulting quilt became a conventional rectangle that made a lovely small quilt (*Figure 5-1*).

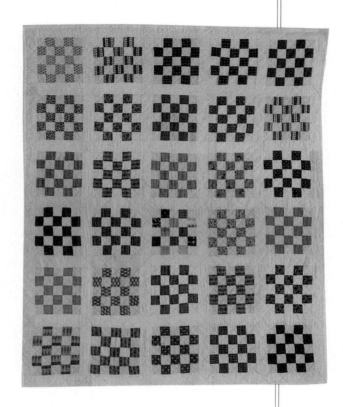

Plate 5-8. *(above right)*
TWENTY-FIVE PATCH,
54" x 64", Time span: c. 1880–1989.
Machine pieced and quilted. When purchased at an antique show, this was an incomplete top with four rows of blocks across and eight lengthwise. Two damaged blocks were discarded and six were moved to make a small rectangular quilt. It was machine quilted with nylon thread.

Fig. 5-1. *(right)*
When found, this unfinished top was four blocks wide and eight blocks long. "Remodeling" changed it to a more conventional size with blocks arranged five horizontally and six vertically.

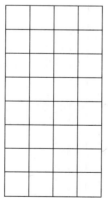
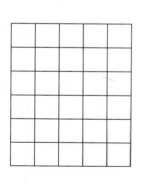

Shape as found   Shape after changes

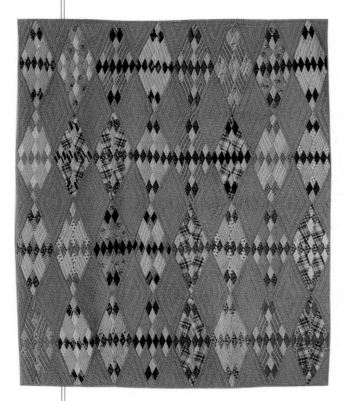

Plate 5-9. *(above)*
TRIPLE DIAMONDS,
63" x 74", Time span:
c. 1900–1992. Hand pieced
and hand quilted. The top
was from an auction in
Phelps, New York. Incomplete,
and an odd shape when
found, sections were moved to
make it rectangular. Pink tri-
angles from vintage fabrics
were added at two corners
and it was backed and bound
with a gray print fabric.

A different problem arose with the TRIPLE DIAMONDS quilt in *Plate 5-9.* When found, the top was an odd shape (*Figure 5-2*) and was obviously a partial top. However, by moving one of the large pieced diamonds from one side of the top to the other side, the basic design was completed. Then, I cut the pink diamonds along one edge in half lengthwise and sewed them to the other side of the top. A complete rectangle was formed, except for small triangles that were needed in two of the corners. For those, I used a similar fabric of the same vintage. The points of the large dia-monds along the edges were cut off dur-ing the process, but the result seemed worth that sacrifice, particularly since the points of the diamonds at the ends of the quilt top were not aligned properly and a few of those had to be cut off to square up the ends. To me, the resulting quilt is pleasant and far more desirable than an odd-shaped, unfinished top. Some would disagree, since this top was about 100 years old, but I saw little advantage to leaving it as found.

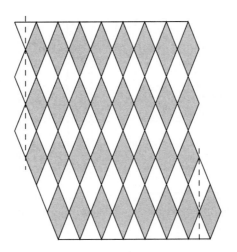

Fig. 5-2. *(left)*
It was necessary to move the large pieced block and half of some of the unpieced blocks to convert this partial top into a usable quilt. Sections moved are those shown outside the dotted lines.

Chapter 6

CLEANING

SHOULD QUILT TOPS BE WASHED?

When someone brings a top to show me, frequently the first question asked is, "How should I wash it?" My answer is always, "Does it really need it?" Most tops have been stored in trunks, drawers, boxes, closets, or other closed areas. Usually they have been untouched from the time they were made and often they appear just like new. Such tops definitely do not require washing.

There are times when a top has a dusty or musty smell resulting from the way it was stored. By far the easiest way to take care of this is to air the quilt top. A *dry* top can be hung on a line out of the wind and sun, or it can be spread on a sheet on the grass. A few hours in the fresh air will usually remove all traces of the musty odor.

Occasionally, a top has been soiled or stained and may need to be cleaned. It is important to note, however, that if any cleaning is needed, it should be wet-washing, not dry cleaning. The solvents used by dry cleaners are not suitable for use on quilt tops or quilts. Important, too, is that for any top being washed, gentle handling is a must to prevent seams from pulling apart and/or fabrics from raveling.

Although many people think cleaning is the first step in preparing a top for quilting, that is not what should be done first, if at all. The first step is to do any repair work needed (see chapters 3 and 4) and only then should one consider washing a top. The same is true for tops that are stained or have discolored for one reason or another; any needed repairs should be made before washing.

COLORFASTNESS

The question of colorfastness is of major importance for all tops, because even if they are not washed before quilt-

Plate 6-1. (above)
HEXAGON,
59" x 78", Time span: c. 1920–1992.
Hand pieced and machine quilted. Made
from a top purchased at an estate sale in
Coopers Plains, New York, this quilt illustrates
what can happen when a fabric is not colorfast. Though one red hexagon was tested and
did not run, others that looked as if they were
made of the same fabric ran badly. The same
was true for the dark blues.

ing, many will be washed at a future date. In my mind that brings up some of the most difficult decisions involved in working with Time-Span Quilts.

Years ago, colorfastness was not so crucial. People rarely washed their quilts but instead used regular airing to freshen them. Today, many people are fanatic about cleanliness and wash everything indiscriminately. Modern detergents are harder on dyes and may cause some to run even though the same dyes would have been stable in the soaps used earlier. Therefore, we need to know whether the dyes in tops are colorfast and should consider carefully the soap or detergent we choose for washing them.

TESTING FOR COLORFASTNESS

Over a period of time, I have learned which fabrics seem more prone to running than others, and though it is dangerous to generalize, I have found that light-colored prints are usually stable, while more intense and darker colors are more apt to cause problems. Dark solids, especially reds and blues, are suspect, though many are completely colorfast. The only way to be sure, however, is to test every fabric.

To do this, use a dry cotton-tipped swab or a soft white cloth and gently rub the fabric. If no dye rubs off, the next step is to place the colored fabric on top of a white cloth, dampen the swab with cool water and check again. Repeat with warm water, and finally try a weak solution of the soap or detergent you expect to use to wash the top. If at any stage the color shows on the swab or on the white cloth underneath, the dye is not colorfast and a decision of whether to wash or not will have to be made knowing that there may be a problem. In some tops the process will involve testing many fabrics, but this is necessary if you want to be certain how the dyes will hold up to washing.

The importance of thorough testing is illustrated by the HEXAGON quilt in *Plate 6-1*. In this top there were a number of red hexagons. Although I checked one, and all of the reds appeared to be made of the same fabric, they were not. Some were colorfast while others ran badly. I didn't discover this until after the top was quilted, and as you can see, the result was disastrous. Some of the dark blues were also not colorfast.

NONCOLORFAST FABRICS

Now comes the crucial decision about what to do if the dyes run. You can either abandon the project entirely, or you can decide to go ahead, knowing the risk. If colorfastness is questionable,

certainly it is better to wash the top to be sure, than to wait and discover the problem after it has been quilted, as I did with the HEXAGON quilt.

If dyes are not stable, consider how big an area the noncolorfast dye involves and how much it seems to run. A large area that runs badly may cause major problems and you may want to abandon that top. However, a small patch might not cause too much trouble. Washing and rinsing the top quickly and spreading it out immediately will minimize the contact of that patch with other parts of the top and may avert a problem.

The FLYING GEESE quilt in *Plate 4-1*, page 48, has several fabrics that run, but they are all very tiny triangles. The quilt has been washed without those problem patches discoloring the areas around them. (The stains on the top are from some other source and I have had no luck at all removing them.)

In some cases, even after testing, an apparently colorfast dye will surprise you and run. If so, it should be treated before the top dries because the dye that ran will become permanent when dried. Try soaking the top in a full washer of cool water to which about one cup of Easy Wash® concentrate (see Washing Products, page 68) has been added. If the dye remains after fifteen minutes, try adding some of the Easy Wash® directly to the area involved and re-soak. This may or may not solve the problem, but it is worth a try.

If there are only a few noncolorfast patches in a top, another answer would be to remove and replace them with other patches of compatible colorfast fabrics. If there are many, this of course may be impractical.

The decision about a top with dyes that are not stable is one you may have to face. It is difficult to give advice or make recommendations, because what you do will depend on the particular fabrics involved and the risk you are willing to take.

WASHING PRODUCTS

With the array of soaps and detergents on the market today, one can be overwhelmed trying to decide which product to use. I recommend a mild product, not one of the many laundry agents recommended to get out heavy dirt and stains. For this reason my first choice is Orvus® Paste, sold by many quilt shops or quilt vendors as "quilt soap." It dissolves and rinses out easily, it is not harsh like many of the newer detergents, it is less apt to affect the older dyes than most of today's products, and it has given me excellent results.

Mountain Mist's Ensure® and Easy Wash®, distributed by Airwick Industries, are other products you might want to consider.

Some textile conservators disagree about Orvus® rinsing out easily, but I have not had a problem when it is used in the small quantities needed to wash a quilt top. At most, a tablespoon of Orvus® in a full washer is enough to clean almost any top. Larger amounts are more difficult to rinse out, but few tops are heavily soiled. Should there be considerable soil, it is more effective to use two wash periods, each with a small amount of soap, than to use too much soap in one wash period.

WASHING PROCEDURES

The worst enemy of a top being washed is stress on the fabrics. This may be caused by agitating the top during the washing process or by pulling on wet fibers while handling and drying it. Wet fibers are weaker than dry ones and need gentle treatment.

It is for this reason that I recommend washing tops in a washing machine unless you have special facilities like those used by quilt conservators. I like to think of the washing process as hand washing in a washing machine. That means a top will be handled very carefully and will be agitated by hand, not by machine.

To use this method, fill the machine with lukewarm water and dissolve a small amount of soap. Use the large load wash cycle for the machine since there is less stress on the top in a large amount of water than if it is crowded into a small load. Add the quilt top and very gently move it up and down with your hands until it is wet through by the soapy solution. Soak it for about ten minutes and then move it up and down again gently by hand to loosen the dirt from the fibers. A long soaking period will not remove more dirt than will a ten-minute period, so for something that is heavily soiled, two separate short soaking periods will be more effective than one long one would be.

After the top has been soaked, spin the wash water out of the machine. Spinning will do little harm to the fibers since it merely flattens the top against the sides of the washer without agitating it.

Next the top must be well rinsed. Add water of the same temperature used for the wash period, move the top around gently by hand in the clear water, and spin it again. At least two or three rinses are usually necessary to remove all the soap, but this can be checked by watching the water that comes from the machine to see if it is clear, with no soapy residue.

Finally comes drying. Stay away from a dryer! Remember, the fibers are wet and a dryer agitates them constantly. A wet top should not be hung on a line, either, because hanging causes undue weight and pull on the wet fibers. The top should be dried flat. This can be done outdoors, if weather permits, by gently spreading it out on a sheet. If desired, it can be covered with another sheet to protect it from leaves or insects or from sunshine, which may fade it.

If the top cannot be dried outdoors, any large flat indoor area can be used. A fan blowing slightly above the top will shorten the drying time. If the top must be folded while drying, refold it occasionally so fold lines do not dry in. Remember to protect the surface under it from moisture with something like a plastic sheet.

STAIN REMOVAL

If you work with a number of old tops, you will soon learn that some stains cannot be removed. For any given top each of us must decide whether such stains are ones we can accept or ones that will spoil the top for us. *Plate 6-2, page 70,* shows two quilt blocks, both of which are stained. The first is most unsightly and is not one I could live with. The second one is borderline. As a block the stain is quite obvious, but if the block were part of a whole top, the stain would be far less noticeable and the decision would depend on whether there were other stains on the top and how many.

It is interesting to me that after a top is made into a quilt, minor stains seem almost to disappear as one admires the overall effect. A quilt mentioned earlier (*Plate 4-1*, page 48) has two rather large stains, but I have shown it to many people and they have not noticed the stains until I pointed them out.

This does not mean you should never try to remove stains, since many can be removed. For overall brightening and the removal of certain types of stains, my favorite product is Snowy® bleach. It is often effective for some of the brownish stains that appear along fold lines or the ones that resemble brown watermarks like the one shown in *Plate 6-3*. Snowy® removed a very large brown stain

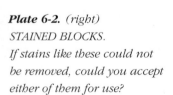

Plate 6-2. *(right)*
STAINED BLOCKS.
If stains like these could not be removed, could you accept either of them for use?

Plate 6-3. *(far right)*
WATERMARK-TYPE STAINS.
This kind of stain is found on many old tops and quilts and frequently can be removed.

of this type from the top from which the quilt in *Plate 6-4* was made.

Dry Chlorox 2® and Biz® are products similar in chemistry to Snowy®, but be careful not to confuse the dry Clorox 2® with liquid Chlorox 2® or regular Chlorox® bleach, both of which are different products entirely and are not color safe.

One must be patient when using Snowy®. It works slowly and sometimes requires a day or so of soaking to show results. In the many times I have used it, I have had only one or two cases where it has affected the dyes in the fabrics or seemed to cause running of the dyes, and I strongly suspect in those cases the dyes were not colorfast to start with.

The DRUNKARD'S PATH crib quilt in *Plate 6-5,* page 72, was made from a top that was so browned with age it was quite unattractive. The top originally had three more blocks on one end, two of which were damaged. This provided an opportunity to experiment, so I worked with one of the damaged blocks first. After soaking it for two days in a solution of Snowy® bleach, it brightened so much that I then treated the whole top. The end result is an unusual and pleasing crib-size quilt.

A different type of brown stain is shown in the smaller block in *Plate 6-2.* Until recently I had always believed such

Plate 6-4. *(above)*
APPLIQUÉD TULIPS,
70" x 73", Time span: c. 1875–1993.
Hand appliquéd and pieced with exceptional workmanship, hand quilted. From an estate in Shelby, Ohio, this top was disfigured by a large area at one end covered with a brown watermark-type stain. Soaking overnight in Snowy® bleach removed almost all of the stain.

stains could not be removed, but a woman in our area who has dealt in antique quilts for about twenty years offered me a solution to the problem. For such stains she uses the dental cleanser, Efferdent®. She dissolves a tablet in about a half cup of hot water. When it stops fizzing, she dabs some of the solution onto the stain, leaving it there to dry. If the stain does not come out on the first try, she repeats the process. She does not rinse afterwards and has never had problems leaving it on her quilts. Nor has she had problems with the product affecting colored fabrics. She has found, however, that on some of the very old white quilts the treatment may leave a spot that is whiter than the original fabric.

I could hardly believe it when we discussed this treatment, but I tried it on

Plate 6-5. (left)
DRUNKARD'S PATH,
36" x 56", Time span: c. 1890–1989.
Hand and machine pieced, hand quilted.
Found in Macon, Georgia, the top had a label that read, "Pieced by D.M. McKey, Grandma Munson." Three blocks at one end of the top, one of which was badly torn, were removed. The top was treated with Snowy® bleach to brighten the fabrics, and a border was added.

that small stained block (*Plate 6-2,* page 70), and it totally removed the stains. It did however, lighten the green print somewhat. I have since used this product successfully on other spots. Admittedly, I have not used it over a long enough period of time to be certain that it is problem free, and I recommend that anyone trying it weigh the hoped-for benefits against possible long-term problems.

Rust is occasionally found on a top, but it can be removed if you are very careful. Its removal requires harsh chemicals that are dangerous to use, so product directions should be followed carefully, safety precautions should be observed, and thorough rinsing is necessary. Two commercial rust removal products are Whink® and Rit Rust Remover®, both chemicals that react to remove rust stains almost instantaneously. The rust is converted to a colorless and harmless chemical, but the area treated should be rinsed immediately to rinse out any excess rust remover. These products will not work on other types of dark spots and are not recommended for any use except true rust spots. In spite of being such strong chemicals, they are usually safe on fabrics and most dyes, but in isolated cases they may remove the dyes as well as the rust, so test a tiny area before proceeding with a large stain.

A word about other stain removers is perhaps in order. In my laundry room I have a collection of over a dozen products, all of which have been advertised as stain removers of one kind or another, and I have tried them all. Results have been uniformly disappointing. I have also been told about people who have had good results trying lemon juice and sunlight, dishwasher detergent, and regular household bleach. Many of these, especially regular bleach and dishwasher detergent, which contains bleach, are rather drastic and are apt to bleach colored fabrics and/or damage your top. My experience has not been good with any of them and I invariably return to Snowy® or Easy Wash® and more recently Efferdent®.

In spite of the ideas above, you will still find there are some stains that cannot be removed. For those, you must make a personal decision about whether they are stains you can live with or not. Stains can be a difficult challenge, but are not always hopeless.

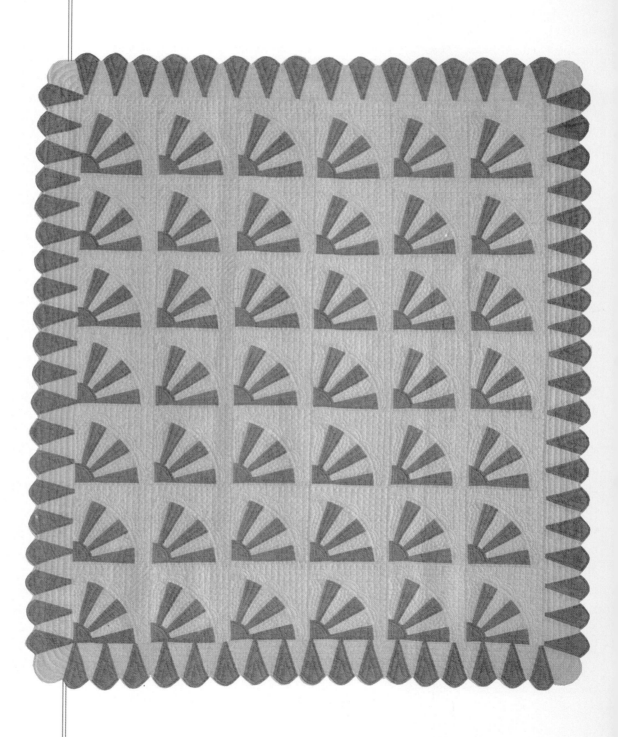

Chapter 7

PREPARATIONS FOR QUILTING

Once your quilt top is repaired and as stain-free as you can make it, there are several other things that must be done before starting to quilt. The top should be pressed, backing and binding fabrics and a filler must be prepared, a quilting design should be planned, and any marking that is needed before the quilt is layered must be done at this time.

PRESSING

After any necessary repair work and cleaning have been done, your top should be carefully pressed. This is important because a top will often be a little larger after pressing and in some cases the difference may be as much as several inches in either or both directions. For this reason, and especially if the top seems wrinkled or puckered, it is wise to press it before preparing the back for the quilt.

Pressing may also reveal problems that might not have been evident at first glance, such as seams that appeared to be sewn but were actually open. I have even found a dye that was not colorfast when I pressed a top with a steam iron. The unstable dye bled through onto the ironing board cover.

Care is especially important when pressing a top that has the very narrow seams often found in old tops, since it is all too easy to pull additional seams open, thereby necessitating extra repair jobs.

BIAS EDGES

Frequently patches along the edges of the top have been cut on the bias and must be carefully handled to prevent stretching. If they lie flat, it is wise to staystitch them to prevent stretching while finishing the quilt. If the bias edges have already been stretched, simply pressing with the straight grain of the

Plate 7-1. (left)
GRANDMOTHER'S FAN,
64" x 73",
Time span: c. 1930–1992.
Hand pieced, hand quilted.
This top from Ohio was
quilted without change and
the edges were finished with a
facing.

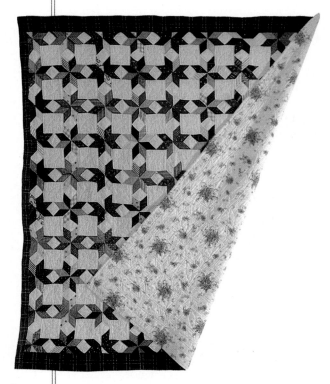

Plate 7-2. *(above)*
EIGHT-POINTED STAR,
74" x 87", Time span: c. 1900–1985.
Hand pieced and hand quilted. Though
included in a group of antique quilts that
came from Kansas, it was obviously an old top
that had been recently quilted. It is a good
example of a top that was spoiled by using a
backing fabric that is not compatible with the
top in either color or design.

fabric will sometimes bring them back into shape, (*Figure 3-3,* page 46).

In cases where the edges have become quite rippled, they can usually be flattened by basting along the edges with short basting stitches and gathering slightly. See Chapter 3, Rippled Edges, for detailed information.

QUILT BACKING

Just as it was important to find compatible fabrics for the repairs or changes that were made in the top, so is it important to choose compatible fabrics for the back and the binding of the quilt. They should compare well in both quality and color with the front of the quilt.

The fabric chosen for the back should be of a quality at least as good as that of the fabrics in the top and 100 percent cotton fabric is preferred, since it is what is found in the majority of old tops.

Many old quilts had print fabrics on the back, but the finer ones almost always were backed with muslin or white fabric. There is nothing nicer than a heavily quilted quilt with a solid-colored back, since then you essentially have a reversible quilt. One side has the pattern and the other resembles a whole-cloth quilt. For this reason my first choice of backing is a solid color, 100 percent cotton fabric – usually white or off-white, depending on which one better complements the top.

The GRANDMOTHER'S FAN quilt in *Plate 7-1,* page 74, is a good example. The back is the same white as the front, and the heavy quilting makes the quilt pleasingly reversible.

Choosing a print can be effective at times but will not show the quilting on the back as well as a solid-colored fabric. Therefore, on a rather ordinary top that will be used mostly as a utility quilt or one that will have minimal quilting, a print may be appropriate. Since a print hides many imperfections in quilting, it may also be a good choice for the back of a quilt that will be machine quilted.

Whatever choice is made, whether the backing is a solid or a print, it should be compatible with the colors in the top. How disappointing it is to look at the back of a quilt and find a fabric that clashes with the front. For a wallhanging, where the back is never seen, the fabric choice is not as important, but the back of a functional quilt is frequently seen while the quilt is being used, so the choice of a backing fabric is important.

The EIGHT-POINTED STAR quilt in *Plate 7-2* is one I bought in a group of quilts, and it illustrates this point very well. The top was made about 1900, but it was finished quite recently. It seemed like a lovely old quilt until I turned it over. The back, which was made from a bright yellow and white flowered sheet has absolutely no relationship in color or design to the front of the quilt and definitely spoils the overall effect.

BINDING FABRIC

Although the quilt is not ready to be bound at this time, it is wise to think about binding fabric at the same time the backing fabric is chosen. This will assure choosing binding that is compatible in color and quality with the rest of the quilt. The EIGHT-POINTED STAR was bound by turning the yellow and white backing fabric to the front of the quilt and it detracts even more from the attractive features of the quilt. (For more about bindings, see Chapter 9.)

CHOOSING A FILLER

Before polyester batting was marketed, quilts were filled with cotton batting, flannel sheeting, and occasionally wool or silk batts. The majority of fillers were 100 percent cotton batts. This meant that if the quilt were to survive successfully without the batting pulling apart or becoming lumpy, the quilting lines had to be less than an inch apart over the entire surface of the quilt.

Many utilitarian quilts that were

made with cotton batts were either loosely quilted or tied. Many of these quilts have not survived well, if at all, but sometimes one is found with a top in good condition even though the layers have pulled apart. Such was the case with the HEXAGONS quilt in *Plate 10-3,* page 108. It was originally a tied quilt, but all the ties had pulled out and the cotton batting was lumped in one corner. After removing the back and batting, the top was found to be in very good condition.

Appearance and Handling

Today we have polyester batting that stays in shape even with very little quilting, and it is especially appealing to many of today's quilters who do not want to quilt heavily. At first glance polyester seems to be ideal. However, if you want to finish an old top so it will resemble one quilted at the time the top was made, polyester may not be an appropriate choice.

Polyester batting was first introduced in the 1950's but was not readily available to quilters until the 1960's. Naturally, it could not have been used for a filler in quilts finished before that time.

The appearance and feel of quilts with polyester batting are different from those with cotton fillers. Cotton results in a flat appearance – whether it is quilted heavily or just a little, and whether the filler is a batt or sheeting. With cotton, there is very little shifting between the layers. Polyester batting, on the other hand, results in a much puffier look and the outer layers will feel as if they are sliding over the batting. An old top quilted with a polyester filler will have quite a different look and feel from one quilted with cotton.

How a filler will hold up should also be considered in making your choice. Polyester wears well, washes easily, and does not pull apart even if quilted sparingly. Untreated 100 percent cotton batting must be quilted closely to keep it from shifting or lumping. Cotton sheeting will hold up well.

Other batt choices include those that combine cotton and polyester fibers, and 100 percent cotton battings that have been treated to prevent shredding and lumping. The combination batts give the look of cotton but require less quilting than 100 percent cotton. In the past few years 100 percent cotton treated batts have come onto the market, and claims made for them say that they may be quilted as far apart as two to ten inches, depending on the particular brand. They seem to work well, but only time will tell whether they hold up as advertised.

Untreated cotton batts on the market

today will duplicate the batts used years ago, but just as their predecessors shrank, so too will new ones shrink. Some manufacturers give directions for preshrinking batts before they are used, but even when this is done, I have found that some of them continue to shrink after the quilt is completed. If you like the old-fashioned crinkled look of many antique quilts, untreated cotton batts may be your choice, but if not, you may want to choose the cotton-polyester combinations or the all-cotton batts treated by the manufacturer to prevent shrinkage.

EASE OF QUILTING

Ease of quilting is another factor you may wish to consider in choosing a filler. Obviously, thin batts are easier to quilt than thick ones. Polyester batts are easier to quilt than cotton. Somewhere in between are the batts that combine cotton and polyester and some of the newer 100 percent cotton battings. Flannel sheeting or double-sided flannel yard goods are, in my experience, considerably harder to quilt than prepared batts.

It should be noted that this assessment of the ease of quilting applies only to hand quilting. For machine work the ease of quilting does not need to be checked. In fact, cotton batting works very well for machine quilting because it shifts less between fabric layers than polyester and it can be rolled tighter and quilted more easily. It is particularly good for machine quilting large quilts.

FIBER MIGRATION

Another important thing to consider in choosing a filler is the fabric used in the quilt top. Many old tops included fabrics other than the 100 percent cotton percales or broadcloths we usually associate with quiltmaking today. In some, the fiber content was rayon, wool, or silk and in others the fabrics were very loosely woven or unusual weaves.

For such tops, polyester batting is a poor choice. Polyester fibers tend to migrate through all fabrics (a problem that is called *bearding*). Firmly woven 100 percent cotton fabrics will resist this migration fairly well, but other fabrics can be very susceptible to it. Therefore, if different types of fabrics or loosely woven ones are included in a top, it is best to avoid polyester batting unless you are willing to include a liner in the quilt sandwich. For a liner, a soft voile or similar thin fabric is placed between the filler and the top and will prevent most fiber migration. I have found that voile does not add appreciably to the difficulty of quilting.

There are also dark-colored polyester

batts on the market today promoted as solving the bearding problem in quilts that are primarily dark. Actually, bearding may still occur but it is just harder to see the dark fibers on the dark fabrics. I feel a cotton batt or a voile liner provides a better solution.

THE QUILTING DESIGN

Probably the most important part of preparing for quilting is the choice of a quilting design since it is the quilting that brings a top to life. The quilting plan deserves careful consideration. A detailed discussion of the quilting design will be found at the beginning of Chapter 8.

MARKING

It is not at all unusual to find old quilts where the pencil marks for the quilting designs still show clearly. Today, most quiltmakers prefer to see quilts that bear no marks, and there are many tools that are available to help them achieve this goal.

My philosophy about marking is to do as little of it as possible and be certain that any marks I make can be, and are, removed after quilting. My methods may not be choices you like or feel comfortable using. If so, select your own, but do plan carefully so you will not leave marks showing on an otherwise beautiful quilt.

Before marking new quilts, we can test markers on scraps of the fabrics used in our quilts to be sure the marks can be removed after quilting. With old tops we usually have no extra fabric or scraps, and marking can be a gamble. Testing on narrow seam allowances is only partially satisfactory.

MARK AS YOU GO

Whenever possible I prefer to mark as I quilt, using a mark that will not have to be removed later. For this reason my favorite marker is a *chalk wheel*. It works well for straight lines and simple curves. I mark with it as I go along, and the marks will have disappeared by the time the quilting is finished. One caution, however – some colored chalks may cause stains. For this reason I use only white chalk. White will show up on almost any colored fabric, and even on many whites, and I have never had a problem with its removal.

There are also *chalk pencils* available. Pure chalk pencils can be used in much the same way as a chalk wheel, but some chalk pencils contain grease that is not easy to remove.

Masking tape is another means of marking as you go and is good for straight lines. Tape should not be left on the quilt for more than a short time, however, because it may leave a residue on the fabric. *Drafting tape* is similar to masking tape, but is of higher quality and is less apt to leave a residue. Any tape should be used only while you are quilting and should be taken off when the quilt is set aside. I remove tape even overnight.

Systems for marking that were used many years ago may also be a possibility. These include *needle scratching* and *soap slivers*. The former is done by actually using the point of a needle to scratch the quilting line onto the fabric. It is done during the quilting process and in a good light the mark can easily be seen for quilting.

Marking with soap slivers simply involves using a thin piece of soap as the marking tool. In the past this was a thrifty use of remaining slivers of soap. Some of today's so-called soaps contain skin softeners or creams that should not be used because they may leave grease spots on the fabric.

For simple designs that are not suitable for a chalk wheel, I sometimes use a pattern cut from a piece of *nonwoven interfacing*, pinning or basting it to the top and quilting around it *(Figure 7-1)*. This method has the added advantage of needing no removal. (Woven interfacing will ravel, so it does not work well.)

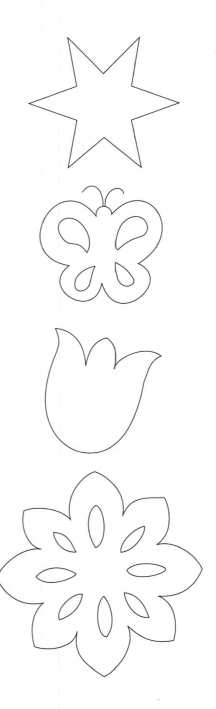

Fig. 7-1. *(left)*
Examples of small, simple designs suitable for making quilting patterns from non-woven interfacing.

Invisible washout markers can also be used to mark as you go along. These markers leave a purple line that disappears after a few hours. They should not be confused with the blue washout markers that remain visible until washed out. It is important to remember, however, that the chemical that makes the mark still remains in the quilt although it is no longer visible. It *must* be removed after the quilt is finished to prevent its possible return at a later date as a brown stain.

MARKING BEFORE QUILTING

In some cases it is necessary to mark the whole top before starting to quilt. This is done before the top is basted and a number of markers are available for this purpose. Depending on the top and the type of quilting design, a light box may be helpful. Because heat can set many marks, be sure to press the top carefully *before* any marking is done.

Regular *lead pencils* have been used for years by quilters, and if tested and used with a very thin light line, they can be removed after quilting. Some quilters like to use a mechanical pencil, which maintains a sharp point without resharping. *Silver and other colored pencils* are available in quilt shops and art supply stores. Although some are quite satisfactory, there are others that cannot be easily removed. Berol's Verithin® silver marker is considered one of the best to use.

Both washout and invisible markers became available to quilters in the early 1980's. The invisible type mentioned previously is not suitable for marking a whole top since the marks disappear after a few hours. Both markers have the disadvantage of making a rather thick line and are therefore less precise than the thin line drawn with a pencil.

Contrary to the opinions of many expert quiltmakers, my first choice when a top must be marked before basting is to use one of the *blue washout markers*. I have used them for ten years and have never had a problem if I always use them as instructed on the package. *It is essential to follow directions for their use exactly* since these pencils can otherwise cause some serious problems, such as staining or fabric damage.

For successful use, the marks from washout markers must not be subjected to heat. Don't press the top after it is marked or leave it on a hot radiator or in a hot car, and don't let your cat or dog take naps on it.

Marks made with washout markers must be removed with cool, clear water. Don't use any chemicals such as soap or detergent in the water.

The marks must be *completely* removed. Don't just dab the top with water, because that merely sinks the marks into the batting or onto the back of the quilt and does not remove the chemicals.

After the quilt is bound, the procedure I use for removing marks made by a washout blue marker is to fill the washer with cool clear water, immerse the quilt, move it with my hands until the water has penetrated it completely, spin the water out, and repeat that process at least two more times. Dry the quilt flat, not in the dryer.

Both blue and invisible washout markers have been used for many of my quilts, including the DRESDEN PLATE and DOUBLE WEDDING RING quilts shown in *Plate 8-1*, page 84, and *Plate A-2*, page 131. They were quilted in 1984 and 1985 and show no problems today from the use of invisible and washout markers.

BASTING

When the top, back, and filler have been prepared, it is important to baste the quilt layers together thoroughly.

The top and the back of the quilt should be assembled with the same tension for both, being careful not to stretch either of them out of shape. Remember that many old tops have very narrow seams so you should not pull them excessively.

There should be enough basting to hold the layers together securely during the quilting process. For hand quilting, a grid of basting stitches two or three inches apart in each direction works well. For machine quilting, I baste with one-inch safety pins, leaving no more than four inches between pins.

Chapter 8

QUILTING

CHOOSING A DESIGN

An important decision in planning and preparing a top for quilting is the choice of a quilting design. To make a Time-Span Quilt appear authentic, you will want to consider the type of quilting that was being done most frequently at the time the top was made.

Although there are no clear-cut dates when certain types of quilting designs were used, some trends did exist. Before the Civil War, very heavy quilting, including stuffed and corded work, was common, and up until 1900 fancy motifs such as feathers and cables frequently had secondary patterns like grids or double or triple rows of quilting in the background areas behind them.

After the turn of the century, quilters no longer did as much heavy quilting, and outline quilting became widely used. Outline quilting involves stitching around a patch about ¼ inch from the seam line.

Outline quilting in the pieced squares was often combined with a fancy motif in the alternate plain areas. This combination was used for the SNOWFLAKE STAR quilt in *Plate 8-2,* page 86.

Barbara Brackman, in her book *Clues in the Calico,* states that quilting "in the ditch," which is quite common in quilts today, first came into use after 1950. This type of quilting is done right in the seam line and the quilting stitch shows only when the quilt is examined closely. It gives a much puffier look than other types of quilting. The blocks in *Plate 8-3,* page 86, show a comparison of outline and in-the-ditch quilting. In the block on the left every patch was outlined with a row of quilting on either side of the seam line; in the other block, the quilting was done in the seam lines (in the ditch) around each patch. The second block is quite puffy and the quilting stitches do not show. The other

Plate 8-1. *(left)*
DRESDEN PLATE,
66" x 82",
Time span: c. 1930–1985.
Hand pieced, hand appliquéd, and hand quilted. This top was made by Ethyl Burke, Rochester, New York, and was purchased through a classified ad. The very plain design was not changed, but the top was converted into a very special quilt by the amount and design of the quilting.

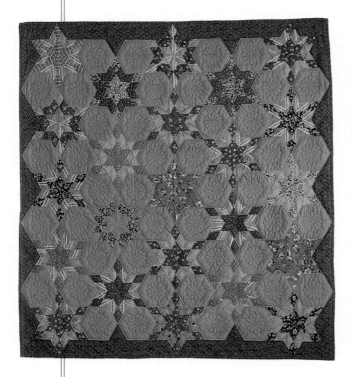

Plate 8-2. *(above)*
SNOWFLAKE STAR,
69" x 75",
Time span: c. 1940–1993.
Hand and machine pieced
and hand quilted. The top
was from Wells Run,
Vermont, and had no bor-
ders. After I added borders, it
was quilted by Helen Heckert
of Hegins, Pennsylvania. Very
traditional quilting combined
outline quilting in the stars
with fancier designs in the
plain blocks and borders.

Plate 8-3. *(right)*
HOSANNAH SAMPLES.
These two blocks show how quilting "in
the ditch" and outline quilting differ in
appearance. The outline quilting on the left
emphasizes the quilting lines and is flatter,
whereas the quilting in the ditch gives a
puffier look to the block.

block is flatter and the stitches do show.

For my quilts, although I do consider the time period when the top was made, my final choice is for a quilting design that seems best for each individual top, whether it is authentic or not. I use traditional quilting designs – such as grids, cables, or feathers – if they seem appropriate, and I also do a great deal of outline quilting, which is easy and requires no marking. On the other hand, some quilting designs that I use are definitely nontraditional.

The PINK MEDALLION quilt in *Plate 4-8*, page 55, and the yellow and black STRIP-PIECED SQUARES quilt in *Plate 8-4* are quilted with nontraditional designs. PINK MEDALLION has diagonal rays starting in the center and radiating out toward the borders. The yellow and black quilt has long, overall waves. The

choice for the pink quilt was made partially because of problems with the fabrics. (See the discussion of quilting problems later in this chapter.)

The yellow and black quilt is a strange little quilt that becomes increasingly interesting the more you study it. It was made by a lady when she was almost ninety years old and it was pieced on papers. Choosing a quilting design for it presented a problem because the patches were so irregular. None of the typical outline quilting, background grids, or fancy designs seemed appropriate to me, and concentric fans or an overall grid lacked interest. Finally, my husband suggested the use of long, wavy lines *(Figure 8-1)*, and the choice proved to be very successful.

Because of the high contrast between the plaids and the yellow background, marking this quilt was a problem; no marker would work well on both the lights and the darks. I solved the problem by marking and quilting it from the back *(Figure 8-1)*.

A mixture of traditional and nontraditional designs was used for quilting the DRESDEN PLATE quilt in *Plate 8-1,* page 84. Since it was a very nondescript top to start with, my son suggested I treat it like a whole-cloth quilt and do a lot of heavy quilting. I quilted the plates first with an

Plate 8-4. *(left)*
STRIP-PIECED SQUARES,
55" x 75",
Time span: c. 1960–1988.
Hand pieced on backing papers and hand quilted. This top was made by Ellen Rouse of Athens, Alabama, when she was almost ninety years old. A missing area at the end of one border was completed. Because the irregular design of the strip-pieced squares made the use of outline quilting or individual treatment of the blocks unsuitable, it was quilted with a long overall wave design.

Fig. 8-1. *(left)*
STRIP-PIECED SQUARES. Reverse side of quilt in Plate 8-4. Long wavy lines were used for the quilting design. Marking and quilting were both done from the back.

outline stitch. Next came the feathers, but after they were done, the need for background quilting behind them became obvious, so I quilted the rays to fill in the spaces and make the feathers show up better. I stippled the centers of the plates, and the final result is a quilt that truly resembles a whole-cloth quilt. Some people believe the back of this quilt *(Plate 8-5)* is prettier than the front.

Sometimes the quilting design will be dictated by some feature in the design of the quilt top itself, as illustrated by the MAPLE LEAF quilt in *Plate 8-6*. Here the sashing varies in width on different parts of the quilt, and it seemed desirable to choose a pattern that would minimize these differences. It was almost impossible to fit typical lattice designs, such as cables or feathers, into the unequal spaces and merely outlining the edges of the sashing did not provide enough quilting to seem adequate. My answer was double straight lines going the length of the quilt. They added interest and minimized the visual differences caused by the unequal widths of the sashing.

Still another factor to be considered in choosing the design for quilting is the original workmanship. The SPIDER WEB quilt in *Plate 8-7* was not accurately pieced, and it is a pattern that has many seams. Where the seams meet in the centers of the circles, the seam allowances were particularly thick and bulky. For sentimental reasons I wanted to quilt this top and decided to just have fun with it, not worrying about the quality of the quilting any more than the maker had about the quality of the piecing. I chose a spiral quilting design, starting at the outside of each block and spiraling inward, stopping when the centers became too difficult to quilt through *(Figure 8-2)*. Only the outer circle of the spiral was marked (with a chalk wheel)

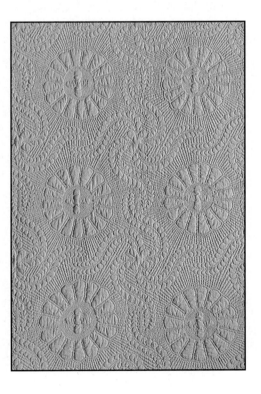

Plate 8-5. (right)
DRESDEN PLATE, detail.
Reverse side of quilt in Plate 8-1. Many people think the back of this quilt is prettier than the front.

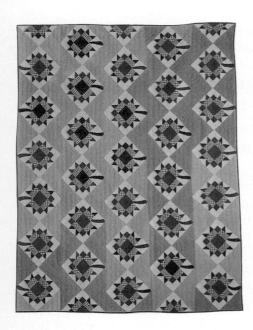

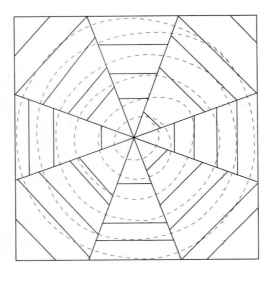

Plate 8-6. *(above)*
MAPLE LEAF,
64" x 82", Time span: c. 1970–1992.
Hand pieced, hand and machine quilted.
Note that the sashing was made from two
colors of blue fabric and varies in width,
presenting a challenge for the choice of a
quilting pattern. A red binding was used to
complement the center flowers.

Plate 8-7. *(right)*
SPIDER WEB,
71" x 84", Time span: c. 1950–1991.
Hand pieced and hand quilted. The top was
found in Cartersville, Georgia. The centers of
the blocks were so poorly sewn that the quilt-
ing was done in a spiral and stopped short of
the bulky center seams. (See Fig. 8-2)

and the rest was quilted by eye.

THREAD

The thread chosen for quilting should always be of good quality. Too many hours go into the quilting process to justify saving a few cents by using bargain threads. Also, threads vary considerably between different brands and choosing a thread that you like and which has given you good results is more important than the brand or fiber content of the thread you use.

The threads most commonly sold today are either cotton-wrapped polyester, 100 percent polyester, or 100 percent cotton. The cotton-wrapped thread is the most common and is made by covering a polyester filament core with cotton fibers. (Metallic and specialty threads are not discussed here because I feel they are ordinarily not suitable for quilting old tops.)

Some threads labeled quilting thread are treated with a coating that is supposed to minimize tangling and make quilting easier. They come in either 100 percent cotton or in cotton-wrapped polyester, but in only a limited number of colors. Although I like and often use coated threads, I have found a few that tangle just as much as uncoated ones.

Top quality, uncoated cotton thread works well, allows a fairly wide range of color choices, and may give even better results than coated threads for people who want very small quilting stitches. Tangling is rarely a problem if threads are cut in lengths shorter than fifteen inches.

Almost all tops more than forty years old are made with 100 percent cotton fabrics, although some do contain other fibers such as rayon and different weaves such as crepe. None, however, contain polyester since it only came onto the market in the mid-1900's. For this reason most people agree that for quilting old tops, 100 percent cotton thread is preferred since it is the same fiber content as the top itself. An additional reason is that cotton threads are not as strong as threads containing polyester and will be less damaging to the top. It is believed to be better for the thread to break than it is for the fabric to tear before the thread gives way.

The color of the thread you choose is a personal matter. Though white and off-white have always been the most common colors used, other colors are sometimes found in nineteenth century quilts. Sometimes dark thread was used for dark areas and white for light areas, just as is often done today.

The widest range of colors today is

found in the regular cotton-wrapped polyester threads. The colors in coated threads, sold as quilting thread, are quite limited and the color range for regular 100 percent cotton and 100 percent polyester threads is somewhere in between. The 100 percent cotton threads may limit your color choice, but the eye blends colors well and *exact* matches are not usually needed.

QUILTING PROBLEMS

Almost all of the quilting problems I have encountered while working with old tops have been due to the fabrics used in the top or to poor workmanship, and when there are problems, it usually becomes necessary to sacrifice the quality of quilting stitches.

Sometimes the fabrics are thin, flimsy, or have an unusual weave that will cause trouble if quilting is done along the grain of the fabric. In such cases the quilting stitches tend to sink down between the threads in the fabric and become almost invisible. There are several solutions, the most obvious being to make the stitches longer.

Another answer is to plan the quilting design so that as much quilting as possible goes on the diagonal. That means that you are going across threads with every stitch and the stitch will

remain on top of the fabric.

Should diagonal stitching not be feasible, and the quilting needs to follow the direction of the threads in the fabric, then the problem can be solved by making slightly crooked stitches. If the needle goes down into the fabric on one side of a thread and comes up on the other side, one or two threads away, then the quilting thread will not sink and the stitch will show *(Figure 8-3)*.

In the PINK MEDALLION quilt in *Plate 4-8*, page 55, I used several of these techniques. The top included a variety of fabrics, including rayons, crepes, and piqués, some of which were quite thin. The quilting design is mostly diagonal, and the stitches are far from the even, straight stitches quilters are

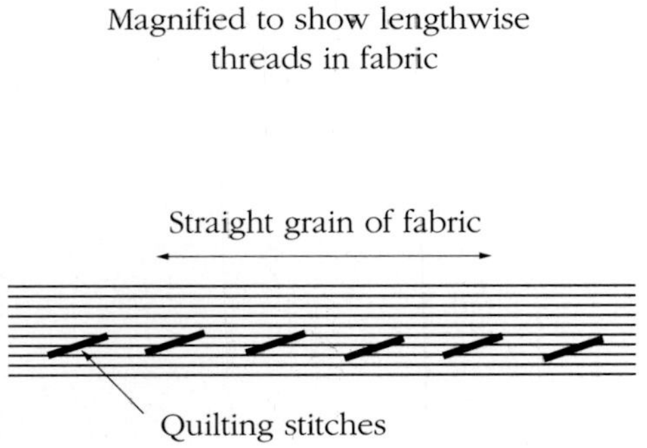

Magnified to show lengthwise
threads in fabric

Straight grain of fabric

Quilting stitches

Fig. 8-3. (left)
Slightly crooked quilting stitches will not sink between the threads of a loosely woven fabric but will instead be held up and show well on the top surface.

Plate 8-8. *(above)*
BULLSEYE,
74" x 88", Time span: c. 1950–1989.
Hand pieced and hand quilted. Borders were
added and considerable fullness had to be
"quilted in" to make this finished quilt lie flat.

taught to strive for, but the unconventional methods worked to give a satisfactory result.

In some cases, the thread count of the fabric is so high that the fabric seems tough and quilting is very difficult. In such cases, it helps to have strong fingers and to choose a quilting design that keeps quilting to a minimum. Many of the background fabrics in the BULLSEYE quilt, *Plate 8-8,* are high thread-count fabrics and they were very difficult to quilt.

Another time problems may occur is when a fabric is brittle. If this condition exists, it is usually in tops over seventy-five years old, and they are ones that probably are best left unquilted. If the brittleness is not discovered until the quilting is in process, it is then essential to lengthen the stitches and do less quilting in order to minimize damage to the fabric.

MACHINE QUILTING

When is it appropriate to quilt an old top on the sewing machine?

Before answering that question, I would like to make it clear that I am a strong advocate of hand quilting and prefer it for most quilts. Hand quilting gives a beautiful stitch that cannot be duplicated by machine, and good hand quilting is very pleasing to the eye.

I would also like to emphasize that my definition of machine quilting is quilting guided by hand on a home sewing machine. This preference is well expressed by Harriet Hargrave in her book, *Heirloom Machine Quilting*, when she writes, "You are not machine quilting, you are hand quilting with an electric needle." This type of quilting is *not* the quilting that is done on commercial quilting machines, but instead is designed and executed for the needs of each individual quilt. Though commercial quilting is appropriate in certain cases today, I do not feel it is suitable for use on old quilt tops.

Machine quilting is definitely inappropriate for older tops since most fabrics do become brittle with age. Machine quilting is much harder on fabrics than hand work and may even cause shredding of some fabrics. Although this does not cause problems in many tops, especially those less than fifty years old, there are times when it may. Therefore, the condition of the fabric should be the very first consideration in deciding whether or not to quilt by machine.

When, then, is machine quilting of an old top appropriate?

One situation in which I might machine quilt is when the workmanship in a top is not good and I therefore don't feel the top is sufficiently good to make hand quilting worth the time and effort needed. The BUTTERFLIES quilt in *Plate 10-2*, page 107, had poor workmanship and did not lie flat, but the fabrics were good and the butterflies were interesting. By using a polyester batt and quilting by machine, much of the fullness was quilted in and the final result is pleasing. It would have been very time consuming to have completed this quilt by hand, and to me the workmanship did not warrant that kind of effort.

Old tops that have little or no design can be finished by machine just for utilitarian purposes. *Plate 8-9* shows such a

Plate 8-9. (left) RANDOM SQUARES, 70" x 83", Time span: c. 1930–1989. Machine pieced and machine quilted. The top came from an auction in Coopers Plains, New York, and was machine quilted for use as a utilitarian quilt.

quilt. In such cases the quilting is done quickly, the resulting quilts are very durable, and they can be used and enjoyed for their warmth even if the design is nothing special.

Another time machine quilting may be appropriate is when quilting is being done entirely on print fabrics, especially dark ones, so that close examination is required to see whether the work is done by hand or machine. If an old top falls into this category, then it might be a candidate for machine quilting.

Sometimes I use machine quilting if I am planning overall grid quilting. Hand quilting of a grid can be very beautiful on a solid fabric, but when quilted on a print it may not appear noticeably different from the same design quilted by machine. Since grids are easily done by machine, machine quilts can be a good answer for grid quilting on printed fabrics. This is illustrated by the quilt in *Plate 5-8*, page 63. The top was made of print fabrics and muslin and a diagonal grid pattern was used to quilt it by machine.

Another time when the finished quilting design will not show well is when the quilting is done in the ditch. One must examine a quilt quite closely to see if ditch quilting has been done by hand or machine, and to me it seems a waste of effort to spend hours on hand quilting that will not be visible. It was very easy to machine quilt in the ditch around all of the sashing in the BLUE-BIRDS quilt shown in *Plate 5-3*, page 61.

For the TULIPS quilt in *Plate 4-5*, page 53, several problems were solved at once by an unusual combination of altering the top and machine quilting it at the same time. Narrow lavender sashing was used to cover the crooked seam lines that resulted when the blocks were assembled. I sewed this sashing on by machine after the three layers of the quilt had been basted, thereby quilting the long straight lines between the blocks and eliminating the problem of sewing through the heavy seams.

Another concern in this top was the fabrics that had been used. The background fabric behind the tulips was a course, heavy weave, definitely unsuitable for hand quilting, and the tulips were made from a rather heavy linen-like fabric. A cotton batting was needed to prevent bearding and that would have made quilting by hand even more difficult. Using a sewing machine and outline quilting solved several problems.

COMBINING HAND AND MACHINE QUILTING

Quilting a top with a combination of hand and machine work may be a good solution in some cases. Machine quilting in the ditch around sashing and then doing the other areas by hand is one possibility.

Another is to quilt the background on the machine and the motifs by hand. The STYLIZED FLOWERS quilt in *Plate 8-10* was done in this manner. The areas behind the flowers were random quilted by machine, and the flowers were done by hand. This top had relatively poor workmanship, especially where the blocks were sewn together, and the random machine work quilted in and covered up the irregularities better than hand quilting would have done. It also went over numerous seams that would have been difficult to do well by hand.

The MAPLE LEAF quilt in *Plate 8-6,* page 89, combines in-the-ditch quilting along the edges of the sashing and random quilting in the background areas, both done by machine. The flowers and the straight lines within the sashes were hand quilted.

One might wonder why the long, straight lines on the sashing of the MAPLE LEAF quilt were not quilted by machine. There are two reasons. One is that hand quilting is more appealing than machine work on solid-colored fabrics. The other is that the long, straight lines are not continuous and would have

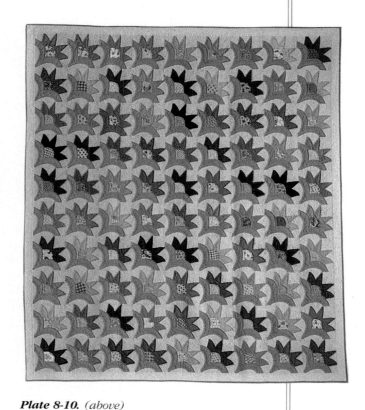

Plate 8-10. (above)
STYLIZED FLOWERS,
70" x 80", Time span: c. 1950–1991.
Hand and machine pieced, hand and machine quilted. From Paducah, Kentucky. Because the seams joining the blocks were poorly sewn and bunched in many places, random machine quilting was chosen for the background areas. The flowers were quilted by hand.

involved a great deal of starting and stopping, a process that is much more easily done by hand than by machine.

When combining hand and machine quilting, it usually works best to do machine quilting in the ditch first, random machine quilting next, and hand work last. In all cases the layers must be basted carefully and, since the machine work is done first, the basting should be done with pins.

THREAD FOR MACHINE QUILTING

The choice of thread for machine quilting should be considered carefully. When possible I prefer to follow the same guidelines discussed previously for choosing thread for hand quilting.

Thread color requires special thought. Because a machine uses two threads, this means, of course, that the thread color can be different on the top and the back of the quilt, which permits you to match the thread color to each side.

For background quilting, the thread on the top is usually matched to the area being quilted. If possible, the thread for quilting in the ditch should match the fabric on the side of the seam where the stitches will lie, but if this is not possible, a neutral color of a medium value, such as medium gray or tan, usually works well.

Grid quilting presents more of a problem since sometimes the grid will go through both light and dark fabrics. In such cases, neither a dark nor a light-colored thread will look right. Sometimes, as for ditch quilting, using a medium value neutral thread will solve the problem, but other times even that won't seem to work. In these cases, where nothing else seems to work, try a nylon thread on the top and regular cotton thread in the bobbin. The quilts in *Plate 5-5,* page 61, and *Plate 5-8,* page 63, were quilted this way with good results.

If nylon thread is used, it is important to choose good quality thread that is meant for quilting. This thin, monofilament nylon can be found in most quilt shops or quilt catalogs. The heavy nylon thread sold in many fabric stores is stiff and could damage the fabrics in a quilt. Some people question how nylon thread will stand the test of time; Harriet Hargrave, who pioneered the use of nylon thread for quilting over eighteen years ago, speaks to this question in *Traditional Quiltworks* magazine, issue #27, 1993. She uses only thread by Sew Art International and her quilts have been used and washed numerous times without problems.

Chapter 9

FINISHING THE QUILT

THE BINDING

By far the most common finishing technique used for the edges of antique quilts was a binding. Bindings varied a great deal in quality and in the way they were applied, and many were sewn entirely by machine. Both edge-turned bindings and applied bindings were also used. Usually with edge-turned bindings the back of the quilt was turned over to the front, but sometimes the reverse was done, with the front being turned to the back. Applied bindings were almost always cut on the straight grain of the fabric until well into this century, when quiltmakers started using bindings cut on the bias. (Instructions for making both applied and edge-turned bindings are given in the Appendix.)

After the sewing machine came into common use in the last half of the nineteenth century, probably the most common way quilts were bound was by turning the back of the quilt to the front and sewing it down by machine. The resulting bindings were usually quite narrow, firm, and neat, and since most of these quilts were backed with muslin, the narrow off-white edge usually seemed appropriate. The disadvantage of these bindings is that they did not wear well, and today we find worn bindings on many of the quilts from this era.

The BOW TIE quilt in *Plate 9-1*, page 98, was finished with a back-to-front edge-turned binding. The top for this quilt was made near the turn of the century and I wanted to choose a binding that would have been commonly used at that time. Edge-turned bindings are easy and fast to sew and, if done carefully, they look good. Of course the fabric used for the back should be chosen with the binding in mind so the colors will be compatible with the top of the quilt. In this BOW TIE quilt, there is

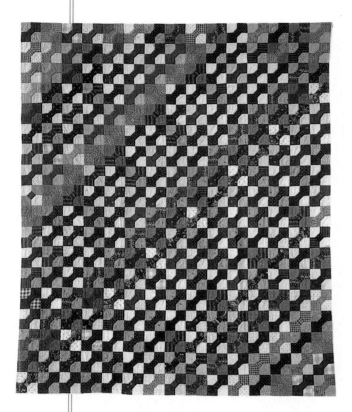

Plate 9-1. *(above)*
BOW TIE,
77" x 93", Time span: c. 1885–1993.
Hand pieced and hand quilted. The top came
from a flea market in Clarence, New York,
and is unchanged. A back-to-front edge-
turned binding, machine stitched into place,
is typical of those found on many quilts from
this time period.

enough white in the top that the edge matches well and actually seems to frame the quilt.

My preference for most quilts is to use a double-fold applied binding (a French binding) sewn as carefully and neatly as possible. It wears well, is easy to apply, and gives an appropriate look. Applied bindings are usually sewn to the front of the quilt by machine, turned to the back, and sewn down by hand. Most of the quilts in this book have double-fold applied bindings cut on the cross-grain of the fabric. Cross-grain fabric has a bit more give than lengthwise grain and can be applied successfully to either straight or gently curved edges.

To complement the quilt and provide a finishing touch without being a distraction, any binding should be compatible with the top in both color and quality. Of course, with old tops we do not have extra fabric left from constructing the top, but we can choose carefully to make the new binding harmonious. Whether a print or solid is used depends on how it looks with the color and design of the top.

The bindings on the quilts in *Plate I-2*, page 10, and *Plate 9-2*, page 99, do not exactly match any fabric in the tops, but they were chosen because they were compatible with the tops as a whole, they are not distracting, and they serve successfully as "frames" for the quilts. The BROKEN DISHES quilt top was made entirely of prints and a print binding similar to the browns in the top was chosen.

The TRIANGLES AND DIAMONDS top contained many solid-colored fabrics, but the best color match for this top turned out to be a brown print that was so tiny it almost appeared solid. In both of these quilts, the bindings that frame the quilts are dark, but as seen in the BOW TIE quilt *(Plate 9-1)*, a light color can work well in some cases.

It is better to avoid commercial bindings since they are rarely the exact color desired and the quality is usually rather poor. A binding made from good quality fabric carefully coordinated with the top is preferred.

OTHER EDGE FINISHES

Quilters today finish their quilts in many ways, including knife edges, prairie points, facings, lace, ruffles, etc. Many of these finishes have been found in the past but are not particularly common. Crazy quilts in the late 1800's often had ruffles or lace. Some pre-Civil War quilts used fringe. Folded triangles inserted into the edge (today called prairie points) have been found on crazy quilts but are rare on cotton quilts before the late 1920's.

Plate 9-2. *(below)*
TRIANGLES AND DIAMONDS,
64" x 83", Time span: c. 1960–1992.
Machine pieced and hand quilted. The flea market vendor said this top came from an estate in either Florida or Minnesota. It was quilted without change except that many seams required adjustment and many areas had to be quilted in. The binding is a very tiny brown print fabric.

Plate 9-3. *(above)*
TRIP AROUND THE WORLD,
83" x 90", c. 1930.
Hand pieced, from Apalachin, New York. The squares that form the irregular edge of this top could be appliquéd to a straight border, resulting in an edge that would be easy to bind.

Therefore, when considering an edge finish for most Time-Span Quilts, the most authentic choice is probably a bound edge. If, however, you find that another edge seems perfect for your quilt, don't be afraid to use it.

IRREGULAR EDGES

When the edge of a quilt is not straight, finishing it is definitely more difficult and presents a challenge. Examples of such edges are in Double Wedding Ring quilts and the TRIP AROUND THE WORLD quilt top in *Plate 9-3.*

Many methods have been used to solve such problems and include work as complicated as binding around each section of the uneven edge to solutions as extreme as cutting the edge straight without regard to how it would affect the appearance. Double Wedding Ring quilts are most often seen with the curves and points individually bound, but it is not at all uncommon to see quilts such as a Grandmother's Flower Garden with the edges cut straight.

One easy answer for uneven edges is to appliqué them to a straight border. To me, this is a better answer for uneven edges than cutting them off straight. For example, the quilt top in *Plate 9-3* could very successfully be appliquéd to a narrow, straight border the same color as the outside row of squares, thereby evening it off and making binding very simple. Edges of hexagon quilts, such as Grandmother's Flower Gardens, can also be finished successfully in this way.

A sketch of another top that had uneven edges when found is shown in *Figure 9-1*, and the finished quilt made from it is shown in *Plate 9-4*. Its small size indicates that it was probably an unfinished top. Since the corner squares were a thin fabric of a different color, it seemed better not to include them in the finished quilt. My solution was to cut the sides straight and use part of the fabric that was cut off to replace the corner triangles. This squared off the edges and made them easy to bind.

Knife-edges or facings can work well for finishing uneven edges, but since they were not commonly used in old quilts they are not considered as authentic as other edge finishes. For a knife-edge, the fabrics on both the front and back of the quilt are folded in and the folds are sewn together with an invisible stitch *(Figure 9-2)*.

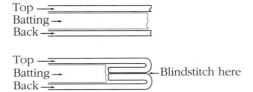

Cross Sections of Quilt Layers
for Knife-edge Finish

Top —
Batting →
Back —

Top —
Batting → ← Blindstitch here
Back —

Fig. 9-2. *(right)*
To make a knife-edge finish for a quilt, the top and the back are both turned in and blind-stitched together.

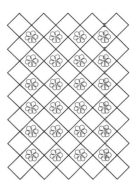

Fig. 9-1. *(above)*
This was the shape of the quilt top used to make the quilt in Plate 9-4.

Plate 9-4. *(left)*
EMBROIDERED FLOWERS, 44" x 68",
Time span: c. 1930–1993. Hand embroidered. Hand quilted by Diane Crisafulli. The top came from an auction in Coopers Plains, New York, and may have been incomplete since the large green triangles at the edges were originally complete squares that made unwieldy irregular edges. (See Fig. 9-1.) Rather than trying to match the background fabric used for the flowers, the edges were cut straight.

Faced edges are sewn in the same way that a facing is applied when sewing a garment. The facing is sewn to the top of the quilt and is then turned to the back and sewn down by hand. A facing gives the GRANDMOTHER'S FAN quilt in *Plate 7-1,* page 74, a fine finish and solved the problem of the small, sharp curves that would have been very difficult to bind.

One complication with knife-edge or faced finishes is that they tend to shift so that the back may show on the front of the quilt or the front may show on the back. To prevent this and to keep the edges lying flat, a row of quilting should be added about ¼ to ½ inch from the edge after the knife-edge or facing is completed *(Figure 9-3).*

SIGNATURE

The final touch for a Time-Span Quilt is to record its history. For this, a nicely prepared label can be sewn on the back. It should give the name of the pattern, if known, and as much history about the top as possible, telling when, where, and by whom the top was made and when, where, and by whom the quilt was finished. If modifications were made in the top, that would also be of interest.

Plate 9-5 shows an example of a label of a top and the modifications that were made to it. Surrounding the written information is a border made from the print fabric taken out of the corners of the original top. The fabric gives a better understanding of why the corners were replaced than any written description alone could provide.

Labels can be anything from a beautifully embroidered or cross-stitched label to one simply typed on a piece of muslin as in *Figure 9-4*. There are permanent fabric markers today that will write neatly on fabric with no feathering into the surrounding fibers. *Plate 9-6* shows a label made with one of these nonfeathering markers. Shown in the same photograph is a tag provided by the New York State Quilt Project, which tells that the quilt was included in their quilt search project. Such information is a valuable addition to information known about a quilt.

In making a label it is important to use a permanent marker rather than

Fig. 9-3. *(right)*
To keep the edge of a faced or knife-edge quilt from rolling or shifting, add a row of quilting stitches ¼ to ½ inch away from the edge after the finish is sewn.

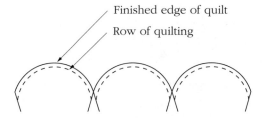

Finished edge of quilt

Row of quilting

something like a ballpoint pen so the label will not smear or bleed onto the quilt and will not be removed by washing. Making either a written or typed label is much easier if the fabric is first ironed onto a piece of freezer paper.

If little is known about the history of the top, you may prefer to omit a label and simply write or embroider your signature directly onto the quilt, telling that you finished it and giving the place and date. Again, be sure that if a marker is used, it is a permanent one.

By all means, sign or label your quilt. Just as we urge people to sign the new quilts they make today, Time-Span Quilts should also be identified with as much information as is reasonably possible.

CARE OF YOUR TIME-SPAN QUILT

Once your quilt is finished, it is important to give it tender loving care. We should remember that these quilts are not made from new fabrics, and the older the original top, the more fragile the fabrics it contains. For example, quilts made from older tops will not stand up to use as bedspreads that will be pulled around or sat upon regularly, but as decorative spreads that will be carefully folded down at night, they should perform well. Just as we would not expect our great grandparents to do the heavy work that younger people do, we should not expect our older quilts to do heavy work. They should be used and enjoyed, but with an appreciation of what they are and the care that they deserve.

> "Lady of the Lake"
> Top made by the mother of Walter Hatch
> of Waterloo, NY about 1890
> Quilted as found by Becky Herdle,
> Rochester, NY – 1984

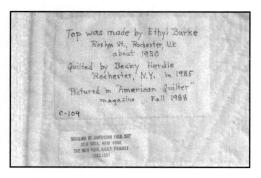

Fig. 9-4. (top, left) *An example of the type of label that can be made by typing on muslin.*

Plate. 9-5. (far left) *LABEL from PINK MEDALLION (Plate 4-8, page 55). The history of this quilt is told in written form but is also emphasized by the border made from the original print fabric removed from the corners of the top.*

Plate. 9-6. (bottom, left) *LABEL, hand printed with nonfeathering ink. Note the small printed label that shows the quilt took part in the New York Quilt Search Project.*

CLEANING

The same procedures and precautions that were discussed in Chapter 6 for cleaning quilt tops apply if your finished quilt needs washing. Gentle handling, minimal agitation, mild detergents, and flat drying all will benefit your quilt if it needs washing.

WALL QUILTS

Some Time-Span Quilts are small and will be used as wallhangings rather than as bed quilts. In such cases it will be necessary to provide some means for hanging them. A sleeve made of a tube of muslin sewn to the top of the hanging is a good answer. If the hanging is symmetrical and appears the same when viewed from either the top or the bottom, it is wise to attach sleeves at both places. By using one sleeve for a few months and then changing to the other, the downward pull on the fabrics caused by hanging is reversed and there is less stress on the quilt.

As is true for any hanging, it is a good idea to take a quilt down and let it rest occasionally. And always be certain that a quilt does not hang where light will fade it.

STORAGE

Although quilts are made to be used, there are times when they must be stored, and in such cases there are two important things to remember:

First, do not put quilts in plastic bags. Textiles need to breathe if they are to stay in good condition. Plastic seals out any air, thereby promoting textile deterioration, mold, and other problems. A well-washed and carefully rinsed sheet or pillowcase is excellent for wrapping a quilt for storage. (Plastic is an appropriate wrap for a quilt that is being shipped or taken to a quilt show, but not for long storage.)

Second, avoid folding the quilt neatly in quarters as we do when folding sheets. If you have looked at antique quilts hung in quilt shows, you have undoubtedly seen fold lines, especially down the center of most of them. This happens because they were folded precisely in quarters time after time and stored until fold lines became set. A far better way is to fold your quilt off center or in thirds, either lengthwise or crosswise, since it is harder to repeat the same fold lines if you do it that way. The stored quilt should be refolded in a different way at least once or twice a year.

Chapter 10

MULTIPLE TIME-SPAN QUILTS

Occasionally quilt tops are found that have come from quilts previously quilted, or there are quilts that for one reason or another would benefit from being taken apart and having their tops reassembled and requilted. Often the latter were originally tied and were used until the ties either broke or pulled out and the batting shifted or disintegrated. Quilts made from any such tops are what I refer to as Multiple Time-Span Quilts.

Just as some tops may benefit from alterations, many of these tops or quilts are well worth rejuvenating – reasons best explained with the following examples.

The SUNFLOWERS quilt in *Plate 10-1*, page 106, was made from a top that had been previously quilted. When found in a garage sale, the quiltmaker had already taken the original quilt apart. This was evident from the scraps of cotton batting still clinging to the back of the top and by remaining bits of heavy thread that had originally been used for quilting. The original quilting had been done along the straight lines between the blocks, but there had been no quilting within the blocks themselves.

When considering whether the top was worth requilting, most important was the fact that the fabric was in excellent condition. By looking at the inside seams, it was obvious that the top had faded considerably during use, but the fading was not localized and the overall appearance was bright and appealing.

No changes were made in the top except to finish removing the scraps of batting and bits of thread. Rather than quilt it in the same places it had first been quilted, the flowers were quilted with an outline stitch, and a small design was used in the areas where the blocks came together. The finished quilt is an attractive example of what redoing can accomplish and probably carries out the

Plate 10-1. *(above)*
SUNFLOWERS,
80" x 97", Time span: c. 1960–1992.
Hand appliquéd and pieced, hand quilted.
The original quilt was made by Mrs. Ralph
Collier of Palmyra, New York, but when found,
she had taken it apart to remove the old cotton
batting. It was originally quilted just along the
lines between the blocks; the new quilting out-
lines the flowers and has a small design at the
corners of the blocks.

ideas of the quiltmaker when she took apart the original quilt.

A good example of a quilt made from one that had been tied is the HEXAGONS quilt shown in *Plate 10-3,* page 108. When purchased, it resembled a sack. All the ties had pulled out and the cotton batting was lumped in one corner. After removing the back and batting, the top turned out to be in very good condition. A border was added and it was quilted by machine to become the stunning quilt shown.

Another quilt made from one previously tied is the BUTTERFLIES quilt in *Plate 10-2.* The original tied quilt had probably never been used, but it had several major problems. It was poorly constructed with a bright magenta border that clashed badly with colors in the rest of the top, and it had a square shape that did not fit any bed size. The quality of the workmanship made it a questionable candidate for further work, but the butterflies had a certain appeal, and it presented an intriguing challenge.

To solve the various problems it was first necessary to remove the ties and the borders. I took a row of blocks off one side and used those blocks at the bottom to change the shape from square to rectangle. (See *Figure 10-1.*) This eliminated one block that was especially poor in

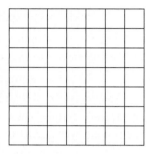

Shape as found

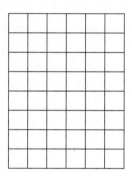

Finished shape

Fig. 10-1. *(left)*
The block arrangement for the quilt in Plate 10-2 was changed from square to a more use-able rectangular shape by moving blocks from one side and adding them to the bottom. One block was eliminated.

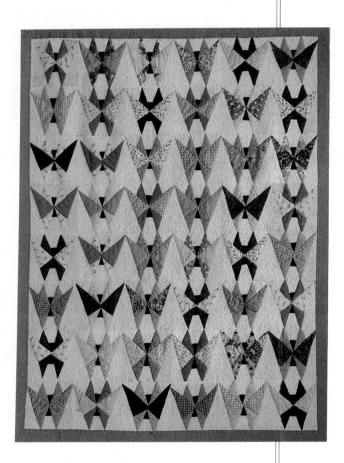

Plate 10-2. *(right)*
BUTTERFLIES,
64" x 84", Time span: c. 1955–1992.
Machine pieced, machine quilted. Originally made as a tied quilt by two elderly ladies in Colorado. It had multiple problems. It was taken apart, the bulky batting was discarded, the shape was changed from square to rectangular, and the original clashing magenta borders were replaced with new ones that matched colors in some of the butterflies. Machine quilting in the ditch was used around the butterflies, and random quilting in the background areas disguised flaws in workmanship.

Plate 10-3. *(right)*
HEXAGONS,
52" x 90",
Time span: c. 1940–1986.
Machine pieced, hand
appliquéd centers, and
machine quilted. This was
made from a tied quilt found
in a flea market in Atlanta,
Georgia. A narrow satin stitch
was used for the quilting to
add color and separate the
hexagons. Photo by author.

Plate 10-4. *(right)*
SUNBONNET LADIES,
76" x 76",
Time span: c. 1940–1992.
Hand appliquéd and hand
quilted. The top had been
assembled into three layers
but was untied and unquilt-
ed. It was quilted without its
being taken apart, but proba-
bly would have benefited from
the use of a batt in place of
the flannel liner.

color contrast. I chose peach fabric for the border to replace the original magenta and to match the colors in many of the butterflies. To help solve some of the problems caused by poor workmanship, I chose a polyester batting and did the quilting by machine. In the ditch quilting was used around the butterflies, with random quilting in the background areas. The combination of a polyester batt for puffiness and close random background quilting made the butterflies stand out and quilted in most of the irregularities due to construction problems.

Plate 10-4 shows a SUNBONNET LADIES quilt. When purchased, the three layers had been assembled and sewn together at the edges, but there were no ties or quilting. Because the layers lay flat, I decided to quilt them without taking them apart, but before finishing the project, I decided I had made a mistake. The flannel sheet used for a liner was very difficult to quilt through, and the backing fabric was a polyester that was inappropriate for the 1930's top. We learn from our mistakes and this was definitely a learning experience. Although it is superficially pleasing to look at, it is not a high quality finished quilt.

The DRESDEN PLATE quilt in *Plate 10-5* was made from a previously quilted quilt. When found, it had very wide white borders that were badly stained, a thin, lumpy cotton batt, a minimal amount of quilting with long quilting stitches, and loose appliqué stitches on some of the plates. Nevertheless, it seemed to have potential, and taking it apart was easy because of the large stitches and the small amount of quilting.

Removing the white borders (eliminating virtually all of the stains), stitching down the loose plates, selecting a polyester batt and a 100 percent cotton backing fabric, and adding interesting quilting turned this abandoned quilt into one that is now very pleasing. Though close examination reveals some of the places where it had previously been quilted, they are not easily seen and do not detract from the overall attractive result.

Sometimes one can only guess whether a top was completed in one or more periods of time. The embroidered quilt in *Plate 9-4*, page 101 may well have been made in two "laps." The blocks were designed so the flowers would look best if the blocks were assembled in a straight set. The diagonal arrangement seems incompatible with the intent of the person who designed the embroidery work, and one wonders if the top was sewn together at a later date by a different person.

So, with Multiple Time-Span Quilts, just as with regular Time-Span Quilts, each one presents unique problems and requires its own evaluation before deciding whether it is worth completing. Given a little imagination and effort, however, many can be rejuvenated and given a second beautiful and useful life.

Plate 10-5. (below)
DRESDEN PLATE,
64" x 65", Time span:
c. 1950–1991.
Hand appliquéd, machine pieced, and hand quilted. This quilt was found in a garage sale, had minimal quilting, a thin, lumpy batt, and a wide, badly stained white border. The long quilting stitches were easy to remove, and most of the stained border was cut off, leaving only enough to provide a front-to-back binding for the finished quilt. It was brightened with a good soak in Snowy® bleach.

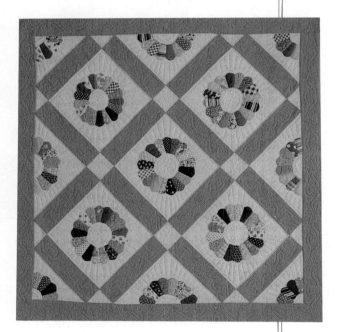

Chapter 11

OTHER TYPES OF TIME-SPAN QUILTS

CRAZY QUILTS

When we think of crazy quilts, our first thoughts are of the spectacular Victorian crazy quilts, most of which were made in the last two decades of the nineteenth century. They were made of silks, velvets, ribbons, brocades, and other luxury fabrics and were heavily embellished with fine embroidery. They were not truly quilts, because they contained no filler and were tied rather than quilted. They were primarily showpieces for women's needlework skills.

After the turn of the century, fewer crazy quilts were made and wools or cottons replaced the fancy fabrics used earlier. For most of this century, relatively few crazy quilts of any kind were made until the last few years when there has been a revival of interest in making these elaborate quilts.

VICTORIAN CRAZY QUILTS

It is not uncommon to find unfinished crazy quilts or blocks that date back to the 1800's, but all too often the quilts are in poor condition and have many disintegrated fabrics. Blocks have frequently survived in better condition than did the finished quilts.

Since the usual way of finishing such tops was to attach a back and either leave it loose or tie it sparingly with ties that did not show on the front, it is easy to complete such tops in that manner. It should be noted, though, that some crazy quilt tops were made with no intention of backing them. The small runner in *Plate 11-2*, page 112, is such an example. The back is neatly done, the edges are hemmed, and fringe was sewn to each end to serve as a finish.

If you plan to complete a crazy quilt top, care should be taken to choose

Plate 11-1. (left)
VICTORIAN CRAZY QUILT,
60" x 60",
Time span: c. 1880–1990. Hand embroidered on backing squares. No filler. Made from twelve square and two rectangular blocks that had been handed down in the family of Hazel Levins of Campville, New York. A few patches of silk, velvet, or antique ribbons were added where the blocks were joined. A velvet border and gold trim were also added.

compatible fabrics and materials just as you would with other Time-Span Quilts. Any fabrics needed to complete blocks or for use in assembling them should be of the same type as those used in the originals. Real silks, velvets, etc., will give the finished top an authentic appearance. Similarly, embroidery threads should be of the same type and weight as those used in the blocks. Pearl cotton of several weights was the most common choice, though many also contained silk and other threads. In the 1800's, the fabrics used for the backs of

crazy quilts were usually silks, taffetas, or similar noncotton materials.

It should be noted that polyester fabrics are inappropriate for completing old crazy quilts. Although they may seem to resemble the old fabrics, when actually placed next to them a difference is almost always noticeable. They are also very strong and may in time damage the older, more fragile fabrics.

The addition of borders is optional as one finds crazy quilts both with and without them and, although some borders were plain, often they were as elaborately embroidered as the main part of the top. Decorative edges like ruffles, lace, or fringe were frequently used on these fancy quilts.

The VICTORIAN CRAZY QUILT in *Plate 11-1,* page 110, was completed from a set of blocks a friend asked me to finish. The blocks were in mint condition and had very elaborate embroidery. The edges of most were uneven, with some fabrics hanging loose. Obviously the maker intended to provide an overlap when combining blocks.

My challenge was to assemble the blocks and add embroidery at the intersections that would mimic that of the original maker to result in a quilt that looked like it had been finished at the time the blocks were made. In the few

Plate 11-2. (right)
CRAZY QUILT TABLE RUNNER,
12" x 40", c. 1890.
This piece has no finished
backing, but the fringe on the
ends indicates that there was
no intent to back it.

cases where it was necessary to add fabrics, vintage silks, velvets, or ribbons were used. Also used were pearl cotton and silk threads of the same weight as those in the blocks and stitches that were similar to those of the original maker. Wide velvet borders and gold trim were added, and a shiny blue fabric was used for the back.

When I returned the completed quilt to my friend, she and her fellow quilters enjoyed exhibiting it in their area, but later she gave it to me, saying that because I had completed it, she wanted me to have it to enjoy and pass on to my daughter, who is also a quilter.

OTHER CRAZY QUILTS

After 1900, the interest in fancy crazy quilts died out rather quickly and other fabrics were substituted for the silks and velvets used earlier. Today, crazy quilt tops made of either cotton or noncotton dress-weight fabrics from the 1920's or 1930's are not uncommon. *Plate 11-3* shows one made of cotton plaids, stripes, and ginghams, an interesting array of fabrics, but a very busy top to look at. Unlike most crazy quilts, it was not pieced on backing fabrics and is therefore somewhat out of shape.

A second top, shown in *Plate 11-4,* page 114, and also made of cottons and

dress-weight fabrics, was organized into blocks, each of which is made up of four randomly pieced crazy quilt squares. With added sashes between the blocks, this top seems more like a modern strip-pieced quilt than what we usually call a true crazy quilt.

Crazy quilt tops made of wool or other heavy fabrics are also found, but as in the previous example they often resemble strip-pieced quilts more than random crazy quilts, and they were not heavily embroidered as were the ones made from fancy fabrics.

Just as with the Victorian crazy quilts, cotton and wool tops were usually

Plate 11-3. (left)
COTTON CRAZY QUILT TOP, 64" x 82", c. 1935. Found in an Atlanta, Georgia, flea market. Note the interesting use of stripes, plaids, and ginghams.

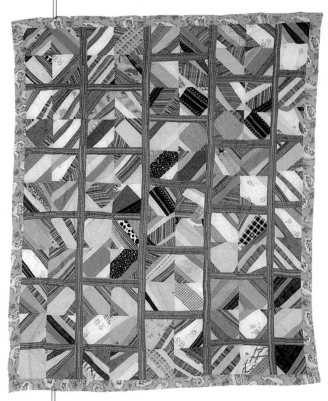

Plate 11-4. *(above)*
COTTON CRAZY QUILT TOP,
72" x 84", c. 1960.
Though the small squares were pieced like
crazy quilts, they were organized into blocks
and set with sashes to give the look of a more
contemporary strip-pieced quilt.

finished by tying them. For the large majority that were pieced on backing fabrics, fillers were not generally used. They may or may not have been embroidered, but if so, simple feather or herringbone stitches were commonly used rather than the elaborate needlework found in the Victorian quilts.

WOOL QUILTS

Occasionally one finds a top made of wool and/or fabrics of similar weights, but usually they are not of the quality of the beautiful wool quilts that have survived intact. Perhaps wool fabrics were not as readily available for making tops, perhaps wool tops that were packed away in trunks or attics were destroyed by moths, or possibly wool tops were more frequently tied quickly and used as utilitarian quilts. *Plate 11-5* shows a NINE-PATCH wool top typical of those that were undoubtedly made for utilitarian purposes.

The top in *Plate 11-6* is typical of many that were only partly made of wool fabrics but also contain many other fabrics that are similar in weight and appearance. It has a planned arrangement of the blocks and bears little resemblance to a wool crazy quilt.

Since the majority of wool quilts were tied, that is an easy and appropriate

way to finish them. Those pieced on backing squares generally did not include fillers, but for the others, flannel sheeting or cotton batts were used. Today a good choice would be flannel or one of the cotton batts that has been treated to prevent its pulling apart easily. Polyester would not be appropriate, not only because polyester was not available when such tops were made, but also because the fibers would migrate excessively through the wool fabrics.

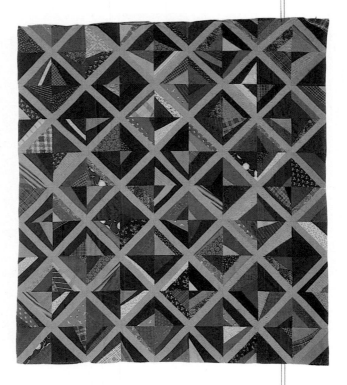

Plate 11-5. *(above right)*
WOOL NINE-PATCH,
69" x 83", c. 1910.
This top was found as a tied quilt with inferior batting and a torn back. The dark, unpieced squares are an unusual loosely woven fabric perhaps used at the time for making heavy winter dresses.

Plate 11-6. *(right)*
STRIP-PIECED SQUARES,
77" x 85", c. 1900.
Machine pieced on backing squares. Made by a resident of Geneseo, New York. This top is not made entirely of wool fabrics, but the others are similar in weight and appearance.

115

Chapter 12

SUMMARY: LEARNING BY DOING

Every quiltmaker starts with a first project, whether it is a pillow or a full-sized quilt, and from then on learns with each project completed. This has indeed been true for me. In addition to basic quilting skills, there have been many new and different lessons learned during the ten years I have worked with Time-Span Quilts. It is my pleasure to share these lessons with you.

As we summarize, please refer to the wall quilt in *Plate 12-1,* since it represents so many of the problems that must be solved and the decisions that must be made when converting old quilt tops or blocks into Time-Span Quilts. If we look back at the various chapters of this book, we can review the steps and decisions involved in making this wallhanging.

Chapters 1 and 2 discuss the real dilemma – to finish or not to finish.

The wall quilt was made from a set of blocks *(Figure 12-1)* given to me by a very good friend. Handed down through

her family, they were believed to have been made by her grandmother at the turn of the century.

Their very old fabrics were slightly brittle and somewhat darkened by age. But the condition of the fabrics, though marginal, seemed usable if handled carefully and quilted lightly. Also, if made into a wallhanging, the blocks would not suffer the stress put on a functional quilt nor would they require more cleaning than occasional light vacuuming. Recognizing and understanding these limitations, it was not unreasonable to work with the blocks.

Were they worth finishing? The workmanship is not of the quality we expect today since many points had been cut off and seams were so tiny they could not be re-sewn. Neither could they be taken apart and re-cut due to the condition of the fabrics.

If only the condition of the fabrics and the workmanship had been involved

Fig 12-1. *(above)*
One block from a set of fourteen that were used to make the quilt in Plate 12-1.

Plate 12-1. *(left)*
*ILLINOIS (variation),
49" x 49", Time span:
c. 1890–1993. Hand pieced
and hand quilted. The blocks
were made by Flora Ann
Magette Cullum (b. 1870 –
d. 1932) in Chanute, Kentucky, and were made into a
wall quilt by the author.*

117

in making a decision, it would probably have been wise to abandon the project. So why did I go ahead? The major factor was sentiment, since the blocks had come to me from a very good friend and had special meaning. In addition, though individually the blocks were only of mild interest, when grouped, a secondary design emerged that was very interesting.

Chapters 3 through 6 involve the preparations for quilting.

Since there were only fourteen blocks, that could not be assembled into a square, I decided on the set used in the finished hanging. It uses only thirteen blocks but still shows the secondary design to advantage. To complete a square, I made border triangles from a new 100 percent cotton fabric.

A bonus resulting from this decision was an extra block, thereby allowing me to test to see if the dark fabrics would brighten when treated with Snowy® bleach. Indeed, they did; however the print fabric was not colorfast and faded somewhat in the bleach so it seemed better not to treat them.

I sewed the blocks together by hand, and in many places found it necessary to cut off points in order to make the seams straight and the hanging lie flat.

Chapters 7 and 8 discuss preparations for quilting and the quilting process.

The backing fabric and batting are both 100 percent cotton..

For the quilting design, because the fabrics were somewhat brittle, I decided to use outline quilting in just the solid-colored areas of the original blocks. For the outer triangles, which are a new fabric, I chose a more elaborate design.

Since I did not want to wash the finished quilt to remove marks, I eliminated the need by "eye-balling" the outline quilting and using a template made of nonwoven interfacing for the outer design. To minimize harm to brittle fabrics, I lengthened the quilting stitches in the old blocks.

Chapter 9 discusses finishing the quilt.

Though not a perfect match for the prints in the blocks, the dark print chosen for the binding works well to frame the hanging. To reduce stress over time, hanging sleeves were added at both the top and the bottom.

Finally, I wrote the quilt's history on the back with a permanent, nonfeathering marker.

Although this summary illustrates the decisions that go into the completion of just one quilt from old blocks or tops, hopefully you will find many ideas throughout this book to help you successfully complete your own Time-Span Quilts.

Gallery

OF TIME-SPAN QUILTS

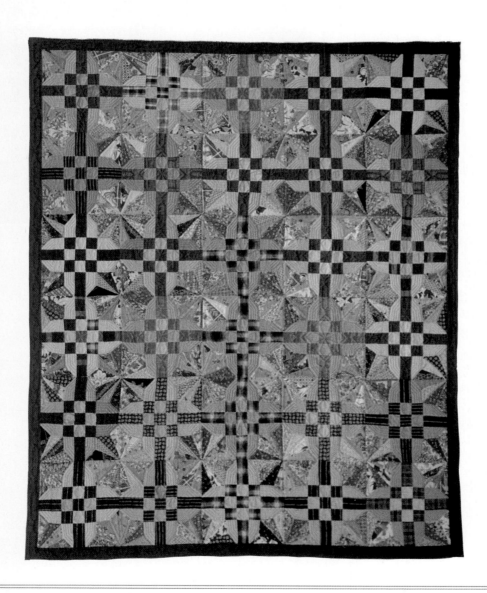

Plate G-1. *(left)*
NINE-PATCH FAN,
77" x 90",
Time span: c. 1950–1992.
Hand pieced and hand quilt-
ed. Borders were added.
Rather poor workmanship
necessitated quilting in and
adjustment of some seam
allowances.

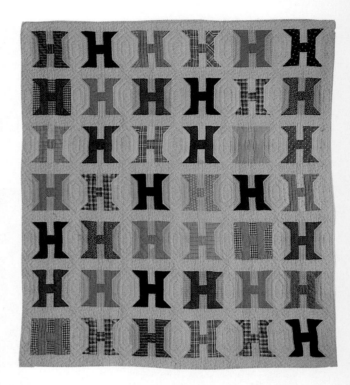

Plate G-2. *(below)*
AROUND THE WORLD,
73" x 73",
Time span: c. 1950 – 1991.
Hand and machine pieced,
hand and machine quilted.
This top had borders on just
two sides. By cutting them in
half, it was possible to com-
plete a border around the
whole top.

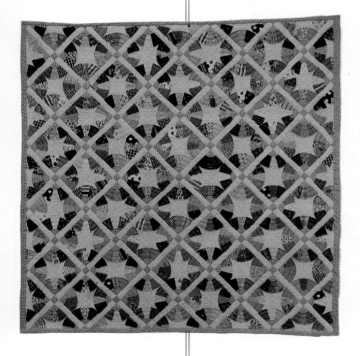

Plate G-3. *(above)*
THE LETTER "H,"
74" x 84",
Time span: c. 1920 – 1986.
Hand and machine pieced,
hand quilted. From a flea
market in western New York.
It is interesting that the blocks
were all pieced by machine,
but the sashes were sewn by
hand.

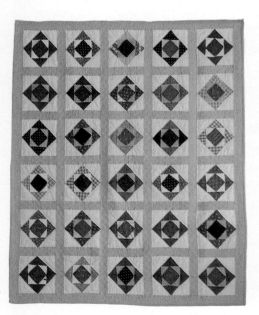

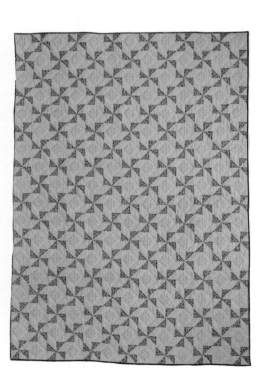

Plate G-4. *(far left)*
TRIP AROUND THE WORLD,
73" x 84",
Time span: c. 1930–1950–
1989. Hand pieced and hand
quilted. The top was made by
Mae Berry in Georgia. The
fabrics indicate that the
center was probably made in
the 1930's with the outer three
or four rows added in the
1950's.

Plate G-5. *(left)*
BASKETS, 68" x 68",
Time span: c. 1920–1993.
Hand pieced and hand quilt-
ed. Quilted and owned by
Dianne Crisafulli, Rochester,
New York.

Plate G-6. *(far left)*
SHADOW BOX,
66" x 80",
Time span: c. 1890–1990.
Hand and machine pieced,
hand quilted. The history of
the set of antique blocks is
unknown. Latticed, quilted,
and owned by Joyce Wight-
man, Camillus, New York.

Plate G-7. *(left)*
PINWHEELS,
62" x 85",
Time span: c. 1930–1993.
Hand pieced and stuffed.
Hand quilted. The top came
from an antique dealer in
Somers, New York, with the
stuffed work already done.
Quilted by Lenore Harvey,
Rochester, New York.

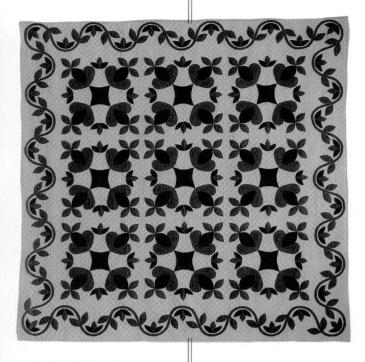

Plate G-8. *(above)*
PINEAPPLE VARIATION,
85" x 85",
Time span: c. 1860–1993.
Hand appliquéd, hand quilt-
ed. Quilted without change
by Anna Farrell of Scottsville,
New York. Owned by Richard
Stokoe.

Plate G-9. *(below)*
PENNY SQUARES,
81" x 92",
Time span: c. 1890–1993.
Hand embroidered, hand
quilted. Blocks were embroi-
dered by Michael Ogilsbie
between 1880 and 1900.
Assembled, quilted, and
owned by Clara Pope of
Syracuse, New York.

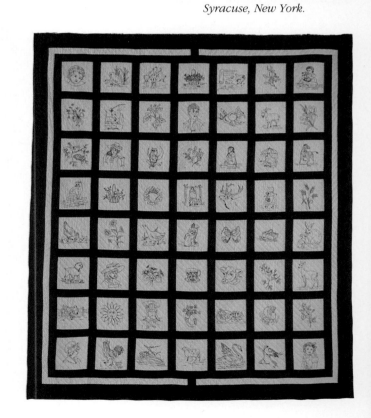

Appendix

BINDING INSTRUCTIONS

DOUBLEFOLD APPLIED BINDING

A double-thickness applied binding is the nicest and most durable finish for a quilt. If these directions are followed accurately, step by step, this binding should turn out perfectly every time and give accurate corners for any width binding and any width seam allowance.

In all diagrams:

represents the right side of the fabric
represents the wrong side of the fabric

Preparing the Quilt

Check to see if the quilt lies flat before starting to apply a binding. If necessary, make adjustments to correct any rippling. See instructions for stabilizing edges in Chapter 3, page 45 (Rippled Edges).

Preparing the Binding

- Choose the binding fabric carefully to complement the rest of the quilt in quality and color.
- To bind straight edges, cut the binding on the lengthwise or crosswise grain of the fabric. To bind gentle curves, use the crosswise grain (it has more stretch than lengthwise grain). Use bias *only* for sharp curves, since it has a tendency to pull out of shape on straight edges.
- To determine the width of the strips to cut, add:
  - a. the width of the seam allowance
  - b. the desired width of the finished binding times two
  - c. ⅛ inch (a fold factor)

  Multiply the result by two to determine the width of the strip you should cut.

  I like to use a binding slightly wider than ¼ inch (⁵⁄₁₆). The following example shows how I used the above formula to determine the fabric width to cut.
  - a. Desired seam allowance = ¼ inch
  - b. Desired width of finished binding (⁵⁄₁₆ inch) times two = ⅝ inch
  - c. Fold factor = ⅛ inch

  Total of a + b + c = 1 inch

  Multiply total (1 inch) times two for width to cut fabric = 2 inches.
- To determine how many strips to cut from a 43-inch wide piece fabric (selvage removed):
  - a. Measure the distance around the quilt top and add 12 inches. (For a 90" x 100" quilt: 90" + 100" + 90" + 100" + 12" = 392 inches.)

b. Deduct 2 inches from the width of the fabric you will use (for example: 43" - 2" = 41").

c. Divide binding length (392 inches) by width of fabric (41 inches) = approximately 9½ strips.

Note: Add a few inches for a very wide binding.

- Measure and cut the strips accurately.
- Join the strips on the diagonal *(Figure 1)*.

Trim the joining seams to ¼ inch.

Press seams open.

- Fold and press the binding lengthwise with the *wrong* sides together.

Fig. 1

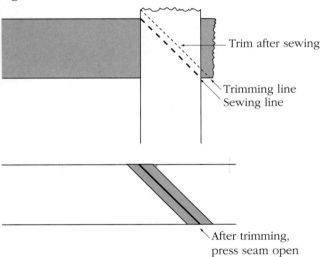

Trim after sewing

Trimming line
Sewing line

After trimming,
press seam open

- At the starting end of the binding:

a. Open the strip and fold the end on the diagonal *(Figure 2)*.

b. Trim to ¼ inch from the diagonal fold *(Figure 3)*.

APPLYING THE BINDING

GENERAL INSTRUCTIONS

- Do not trim the batting or the backing at this time.
- Select a place to start binding, *not* at a corner.
- Plan the placement of the binding so seams do not come at a corner. (If necessary, cut and re-seam.)
- Remember to use the seam allowance that was planned when figuring the width of the binding strip.
- Watch the grain of the quilt, front and back, smoothing all layers to the sides to prevent any pulling.
- Be careful not to stretch the binding while applying.
- Sew the binding first to the front of the quilt by machine; then fold it over to the back and finish with a blindstitch by hand.
- Be accurate.

Fig. 2

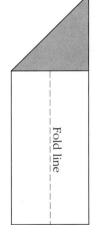

Fold line

Fig. 3

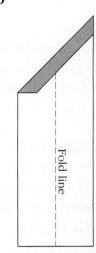

Fold line

DETAILED INSTRUCTIONS

• Start applying the binding with the fold open *(Figure 4)*. Sew one thickness of the binding to the quilt for 3 to 4 inches, keeping the raw edge of the binding lined up with the edge of the quilt top.

Fig. 4

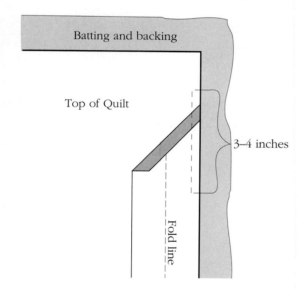

Batting and backing

Top of Quilt

3–4 inches

Fold line

• Fold the binding into the doubled position and sew the remaining distance around the quilt through both thicknesses *(Figure 5)*.

• At the corners:

    a. Determine the exact point where the seam should turn the corner – Point A *(Figure 6)*.

    b. Sew the binding *exactly* to Point A. Backstitch and remove the work from the machine.

    c. Turn the work and measure the exact distance from Point A to the folded edge of the binding – Point B *(Figure 7)*.

Fig. 5

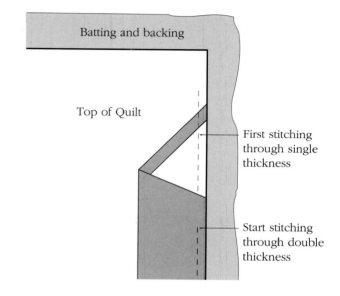

Batting and backing

Top of Quilt

First stitching through single thickness

Start stitching through double thickness

Fig. 6

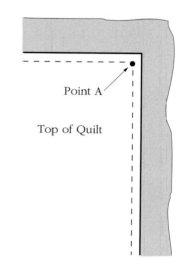

Point A

Top of Quilt

d. Measure this exact same distance from Point A out onto the unsewn binding – Point C *(Figure 7)*.
(The distances from A to B and from A to C are identical.)

e. To make the corner-fold, insert a pin down through the binding at Point C. Hold it and turn the loose binding enough so that the point of the pin can then be inserted into the quilt exactly at Point A. Then as the unsewn binding is positioned to continue down the unbound side of the quilt, keep the pin snugly in place to hold Point C over Point A, and the corner fold will fall into place *(Figure 8)*.

f. Insert the needle at Point C without catching the fold of the binding. (The needle should go as closely as possible into the point where the pin was holding Point C and A together.)

g. Sew with a shortened stitch length for several stitches to fasten the thread and then continue to stitch with a regular stitch length down the next side.

• When you return to the starting point, place the end of the binding over the single thickness sewn at the start. Cut off any excess binding so that the end of the binding will tuck into the pocket formed at the starting point. Fold the loose side of the starting binding over into position and stitch through all thicknesses.

FINISHING THE BINDING

• Trim away the excess batting and backing. Be sure to leave enough batting to completely fill the finished binding.
• Blindstitch the diagonal overlap at the start/end point.
• Fold the binding to the back and blind or slipstitch it into place, just covering the machine stitching line. Use small, inconspicuous stitches and a thread color that matches the binding.
• At the corners, sew right up to the turning point before folding the miters into position. Blindstitch the miters on the front and back and continue down the next side.

Fig. 7

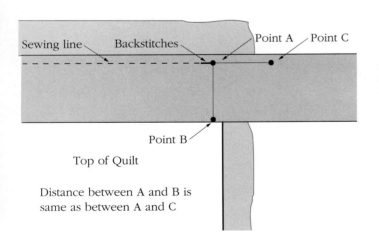

Sewing line   Backstitches   Point A   Point C

Point B

Top of Quilt

Distance between A and B is same as between A and C

Fig. 8

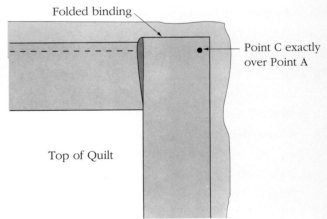

Folded binding

Point C exactly over Point A

Top of Quilt

BINDING INSIDE CORNERS

Because most quilts are square or rectangular, they have right-angle corners that are easily bound by the directions for a doublefold applied binding. Quilts such as Double Wedding Ring and Grandmother's Flower Garden quilts present a different challenge – inside corners. All too often we see the bindings on such quilts stretched or bunched around the corners even though a perfect turn with neat miters on both the front and back is possible.

DIRECTIONS

Prepare a doublefold binding and attach it in the same way previously described, except for the inside corners. If you are binding a curved edge, such as a Double Wedding Ring quilt, be sure to use a binding that is cut on the cross grain of the fabric. It gives enough stretch for narrow, gently curved bindings.

INSIDE CORNERS

• Determine exactly where the binding seam should turn at the corner – Point A *(Figure 9)*.

Fig. 9

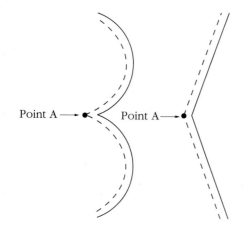

Point A ← •   Point A ← •

• Shorten the stitches to a fine stitch length for about ½ inch on either side of the turning Point A.
• Stitch exactly to Point A, stopping with the needle in the work, and raise the presser foot.
• Turn the sides of the quilt so the edges line up in a straight line with the binding lying flat along the edge *(Figure 10)*. The quilt will be bunched up to the left behind the needle.

Fig. 10

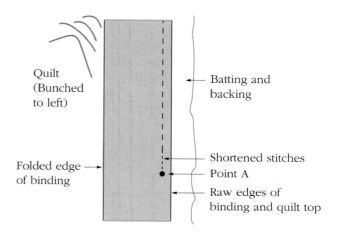

Quilt (Bunched to left)

Batting and backing

Folded edge of binding

Shortened stitches

Point A

Raw edges of binding and quilt top

• Lower the presser foot and continue stitching, being careful not to catch the bunched up quilt or to stretch the binding. Use fine stitches for ½ inch before lengthening them again.
• Continue binding around the quilt repeating steps 1 to 5 at each inside corner.
• Trim the batting and backing fabric and turn the binding to the back. Stitch in place as in the previous directions except that before getting to each inside corner,

the *binding* fabric should be notched in the seam allowance between the raw edge and turning Point A *(Figure 11)*.

- When the binding is turned to the back and stitched down, the miters will fall into place on both front and back. Blindstitch them as you go along.

Fig. 11

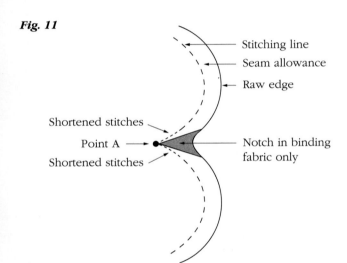

Stitching line
Seam allowance
Raw edge
Shortened stitches
Point A
Shortened stitches
Notch in binding fabric only

Fig. 12

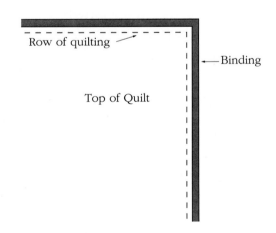

Row of quilting
Binding
Top of Quilt

EDGE-TURNED BINDINGS

Many quilts are not bound with an applied binding, but instead the fabric from one side of the quilt is folded around to the other side, encasing the edge and serving as the quilt's binding. Such bindings are called edge-turned bindings. It is far more common for the back of the quilt to be folded around to the front, but in some cases the front is turned to the back.

Because this edge has just one thickness of fabric, it is not as durable as a double-fold binding, but if done well, it can be just as attractive. Unfortunately, we sometimes see lovely, hand-quilted quilts bound this way but discover upon looking closely that the binding seems loose and shifts along the edge although it has been nicely sewn where it is attached to the quilt. This shifting occurs because the binding has not been secured through all three layers of the quilt. Sometimes, too, this type of binding may not harmonize in color or quality with the fabrics and design on the top.

Avoiding the latter problem involves early planning. If a back-to-front binding is to be used, then the backing fabric should be chosen at the same time as the fabrics for the top. Since it will show as the binding on the front, it should look like an integral part of the design – in quality, color, and the width that shows.

The problem of loose, shifting edges involves the final sewing of the binding. On a hand-quilted quilt, shifting is best prevented by quilting right along the edge of the binding *(Figure 12)*. This secures the three layers, prevents shifting, and gives a finished appearance. Another answer is to catch all three layers of the quilt while sewing the binding to the front. This may be a bit faster than adding a row of quilting, but it is hard to do well and is less durable than a line of quilting.

For a machine-quilted or tied quilt, the edge-turned binding may be sewn in place by machine through all layers, which will give a firm, neat edge that closely resembles an applied binding.

PLAN AHEAD

- Choose a backing fabric that harmonizes in quality and color with the fabric and design of the quilt top.
- Before basting the quilt layers together, be sure each corner of the quilt top is square.
- Allow enough backing fabric on all four sides for the binding (at least twice the width of the finished binding).

THE BINDING STEPS

- Trim the batting even with the quilt top, being careful not to cut the backing fabric.
- Baste all around the quilt. Baste ¼ inch from the edge to prevent slippage of the layers.
- Trim the backing fabric so its distance from the edge of the quilt top equals twice the desired width of the finished binding (*Figure 13*).
- Mark the point (Point A) where the finished binding will turn at the corner (*Figure 13*).
- Fold the corner of the back exactly across the corner of the quilt top forming a right triangle (*Figure 14*). Finger press, being careful not to stretch the bias fold.

Fig. 13

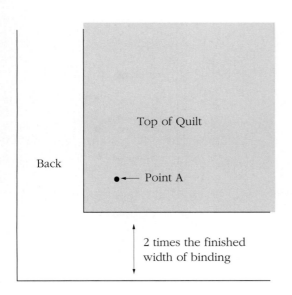

Top of Quilt

Back

• ← Point A

2 times the finished
width of binding

Fig. 14

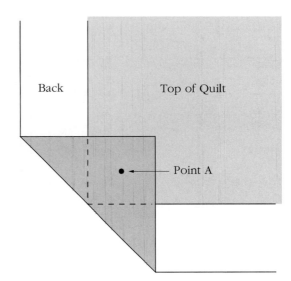

Back

Top of Quilt

• ← Point A

Fig. 15

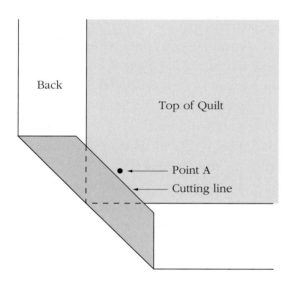

Fig. 16

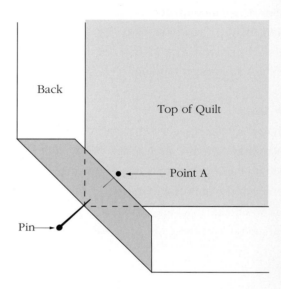

Fig. 17

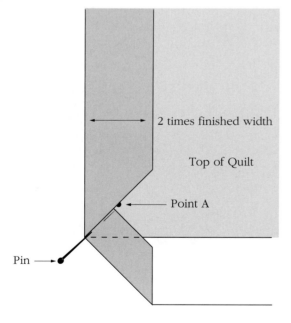

Fig. 18

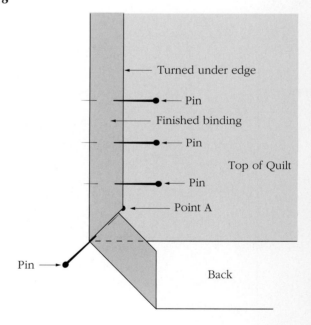

- Cut off the excess fabric between the fold and Point A *(Figure 15)*.
- Pin the fold in place, using a long pin lined up between the corner of the quilt and Point A *(Figure 16)*.
- Bring the back over to the front so the folded edge at the corner lines up with the long pin *(Figure 17)*. Be careful when turning not to pull the fabric off-grain. Repeat for the other side of the corner.
- Turn the raw edges under along all sides and pin securely *(Figure 18)*.
- Sew the binding in place:
    a. Blindstitch the miters.
    b. Sew the edges by hand or machine as appropriate.
    c. If sewn by hand, add a line of quilting close to the edge of the binding *(Figure 12,* page 128*)*.
- Remove basting added in second step.

Plate A-2. *(above)*
DOUBLE WEDDING RING, detail,
70" x 100", Time span: c. 1930–1984.
Sample of binding inside corner. Hand pieced and hand quilted. The top was made by Ethyl Burke of Rochester, New York, and is unchanged. Two different original quilting designs were used and the applied binding follows the irregular shape of the Wedding Ring edge.

Plate A-1. *(above)*
STYLIZED FLOWERS, detail.
Sample of double-fold binding. Full quilt shown in Plate 8-10, page 95.

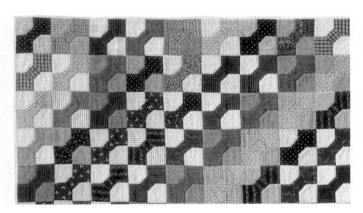

Plate A-3. *(above)*
BOW TIE, detail.
Sample of edge-turned binding. Full quilt shown in Plate 9-1, page 98.

BIBLIOGRAPHY

Many of these references were prepared for and apply particularly to quilts, but they contain a great deal of information that applies equally well to old quilt tops. You will discover as you explore them, however, that in many cases my philosophies and methods differ from those presented by the various authors.

ARTICLES

Brackman, Barbara. "Old Tops: To Quilt or Not?," *Quilter's Newsletter Magazine,* May 1986: pp. 26–27.

Brackman, Barbara. "Techniques for Quilting and Finishing Old Tops," *Quilter's Newsletter Magazine,* June 1986: pp. 20–21.

Hargrave, Harriet. "Care of Today's Quilts," *Traditional Quiltworks,* No. 3, 1989: pp. 47–48.

Hargrave, Harriet. *Traditional Quiltworks,* No. 27, 1993: p. 67.

McElderry, Shirley. "Repairing Older Quilts & Tops," *American Quilter,* Vol VIII, No. 1, Spring 1992: pp. 38–40.

Orlofsky, Patty. "Collector's Guide for the Care of Quilts in the Home," Textile Conservation Workshop, Main Street, South Salem, New York.

Phillippi, Barbara. "Pre-1940 Quilt Tops: Their Status and Fate in Western New York State," *Uncoverings 1990,* Volume 11 of the Research Papers of the American Quilt Study Group.

Slama, Carol Edith. "Quilt Conservation: the Business of History," *The Professional Quilter Magazine,* Feb. 1989: pp. 8–9.

BOOKS

Atkins, Jacqueline M., and Phyllis A Tepper. *New York Beauties.* Dutton Studio Books, 1992.

Brackman, Barbara. *Clues in the Calico.* EPM Publications, Inc., 1989.

Brackman, Barbara. *Encyclopedia of Pieced Quilt Patterns.* American Quilter's Society, 1993.

Hargrave, Harriet. *Heirloom Machine Quilting.* C & T Publishing, 1990.

Holstein, Jonathan. *The Pieced Quilt, an American Design Tradition.* Galahad Books, 1973.

Joseph, Marjory L. *Essentials of Textiles,* 2nd Edition. Holt, Rinehart & Winston, 1980.

Khin, Yvonne M. *The Collector's Dictionary of Quilt Names & Patterns.* Acropolis Books LTD, 1980.

Martin, Nancy J. *Pieces of the Past.* That Patchwork Place, Inc., 1986.

McMorris, Penny. *Crazy Quilt.* E.P. Dutton, Inc., 1984.

Nephew, Sara. *My Mother's Quilts.* That Patchwork Place, 1988.

Puertes, Nancy O'Bryant. *First Aid for Family Quilts.* Moon over the Mountain Publishing Co., 1986.

Waldvogel, Merikay. *Soft Covers for Hard Times.* Rutledge Hill Press, 1990.

Woodard, Thos. K. & Blanche Greenstein. *Twentieth Century Quilts 1900–1950.* E.P. Dutton, 1988.

Index of Quilt Tops

Index of Time-Span Quilts

About the Author

Born in Atlanta, Georgia, Becky Herdle came to upstate New York for college and afterwards to work in Rochester, New York, where she met her husband, Lloyd. They have six children and eight grandchildren.

Although she was taught to sew by her mother, Becky knew nothing about quilts until 1977 when her work as a 4-H leader involved her in a brief quiltmaking training class. It was still another course about patchwork on the sewing machine, however, that really caught her interest and from then on, quilting became an important part of her life.

Through the years she has made a number of quilts, preferring to work with traditional patterns and making them unusual through her placement of colors.

Becky is an author, instructor, lecturer, and NQA certified judge whose work and articles have been published in various magazines and books. She has judged quilt shows at the local, state, regional, and national levels and has received many ribbons and awards for her work.

At the time Becky first started quilting, she and her daughter were selling small items in craft shows, so her time for creating quilts was limited. Her evenings, however, were free for quilting and that was when she began quilting old quilt tops. In a period of ten years, she has finished close to fifty quilts from old tops and shares in this book many of the things she has learned in the process.

American Quilter's Society

dedicated to publishing books for today's quilters

The following AQS publications are currently available:

- **Adapting Architectural Details for Quilts,** Carol Wagner, #2282: AQS, 1991, 88 pages, softbound, $12.95
- **American Beauties: Rose & Tulip Quilts,** Gwen Marston & Joe Cunningham, #1907: AQS, 1988, 96 pages, softbound, $14.95
- **America's Pictorial Quilts,** Caron L. Mosey, #1662: AQS, 1985, 112 pages, hardbound, $19.95
- **Appliqué Designs: My Mother Taught Me to Sew,** Faye Anderson, #2121: AQS, 1990, 80 pages, softbound, $12.95
- **Appliqué Patterns from Native American Beadwork Designs,** Dr. Joyce Mori, #3790: AQS, 1994, 96 pages, softbound, $14.95
- **Arkansas Quilts: Arkansas Warmth,** Arkansas Quilter's Guild, Inc., #1908: AQS, 1987, 144 pages, hardbound, $24.95
- **The Art of Hand Appliqué,** Laura Lee Fritz, #2122: AQS, 1990, 80 pages, softbound, $14.95
- **...Ask Helen More About Quilting Designs,** Helen Squire, #2099: AQS, 1990, 54 pages, 17 x 11, spiral-bound, $14.95
- **Award-Winning Quilts & Their Makers, Vol. I: The Best of AQS Shows – 1985-1987,** #2207: AQS, 1991, 232 pages, softbound, $24.95
- **Award-Winning Quilts & Their Makers, Vol. II: The Best of AQS Shows – 1988-1989,** #2354: AQS, 1992, 176 pages, softbound, $24.95
- **Award-Winning Quilts & Their Makers, Vol. III: The Best of AQS Shows – 1990-1991,** #3425: AQS, 1993, 180 pages, softbound, $24.95
- **Award-Winning Quilts & Their Makers, Vol. IV: The Best of AQS Shows – 1992-1993,** #3791: AQS, 1994, 180 pages, softbound, $24.95
- **Classic Basket Quilts,** Elizabeth Porter & Marianne Fons, #2208: AQS, 1991, 128 pages, softbound, $16.95
- **A Collection of Favorite Quilts,** Judy Florence, #2119: AQS, 1990, 136 pages, softbound, $18.95
- **Creative Machine Art,** Sharee Dawn Roberts, #2355: AQS, 1992, 142 pages, 9 x 9, softbound, $24.95
- **Dear Helen, Can You Tell Me?...All about Quilting Designs,** Helen Squire, #1820: AQS, 1987, 51 pages, 17 x 11, spiral-bound, $12.95
- **Double Wedding Ring Quilts: New Quilts from an Old Favorite,** #3870: AQS, 1994, 112 pages, softbound, $14.95
- **Dye Painting!,** Ann Johnston, #3399: AQS, 1992, 88 pages, softbound, $19.95
- **Dyeing & Overdyeing of Cotton Fabrics,** Judy Mercer Tescher, #2030: AQS, 1990, 54 pages, softbound, $9.95
- **Encyclopedia of Pieced Quilt Patterns,** compiled by Barbara Brackman, #3468: AQS, 1993, 552 pages, hardbound, $34.95
- **Flavor Quilts for Kids to Make: Complete Instructions for Teaching Children to Dye, Decorate & Sew Quilts,** Jennifer Amor, #2356: AQS, 1991, 120 pages, softbound, $12.95
- **From Basics to Binding: A Complete Guide to Making Quilts,** Karen Kay Buckley, #2381: AQS, 1992, 160 pages, softbound, $16.95
- **Fun & Fancy Machine Quiltmaking,** Lois Smith, #1982: AQS, 1989, 144 pages, softbound, $19.95
- **Gallery of American Quilts 1830-1991: Book III,** #3421: AQS, 1992, 128 pages, softbound, $19.95
- **The Grand Finale: A Quilter's Guide to Finishing Projects,** Linda Denner, #1924: AQS, 1988, 96 pages, softbound, $14.95
- **Heirloom Miniatures,** Tina M. Gravatt, #2097: AQS, 1990, 64 pages, softbound, $9.95
- **Infinite Stars,** Gayle Bong, #2283: AQS, 1992, 72 pages, softbound, $12.95
- **The Ins and Outs: Perfecting the Quilting Stitch,** Patricia J. Morris, #2120: AQS, 1990, 96 pages, softbound, $9.95
- **Irish Chain Quilts: A Workbook of Irish Chains & Related Patterns,** Joyce B. Peaden, #1906: AQS, 1988, 96 pages, softbound, $14.95
- **Jacobean Appliqué: Book I, "Exotica,"** Patricia B. Campbell & Mimi Ayars, Ph.D, #3784: AQS, 1993, 160 pages, softbound, $18.95
- **The Judge's Task: How Award-Winning Quilts Are Selected,** Patricia J. Morris, #3904: AQS, 1993, 128 pages, softbound, $19.95
- **The Log Cabin Returns to Kentucky: Quilts from the Pilgrim/Roy Collection,** Gerald Roy and Paul Pilgrim, #3329: AQS, 1992, 36 pages, 9 x 7, softbound, $12.95
- **Marbling Fabrics for Quilts: A Guide for Learning & Teaching,** Kathy Fawcett & Carol Shoaf, #2206: AQS, 1991, 72 pages, softbound, $12.95
- **More Projects and Patterns: A Second Collection of Favorite Quilts,** Judy Florence, #3330: AQS, 1992, 152 pages, softbound, $18.95
- **Nancy Crow: Quilts and Influences,** Nancy Crow, #1981: AQS, 1990, 256 pages, 9 x 12, hardcover, $29.95
- **Nancy Crow: Work in Transition,** Nancy Crow, #3331: AQS, 1992, 32 pages, 9 x 10, softbound, $12.95
- **New Jersey Quilts – 1777 to 1950: Contributions to an American Tradition,** The Heritage Quilt Project of New Jersey; text by Rachel Cochran, Rita Erickson, Natalie Hart & Barbara Schaffer, #3332: AQS, 1992, 256 pages, softbound, $29.95
- **No Dragons on My Quilt,** Jean Ray Laury with Ritva Laury & Lizabeth Laury, #2153: AQS, 1990, 52 pages, hardcover, $12.95
- **Oklahoma Heritage Quilts,** Oklahoma Quilt Heritage Project #2032: AQS, 1990, 144 pages, softbound, $19.95
- **Old Favorites in Miniature,** Tina Gravatt #3469: AQS, 1993, 104 pages, softbound, $15.95
- **A Patchwork of Pieces: An Anthology of Early Quilt Stories 1845-1940,** complied by Cuesta Ray Benberry and Carol Pinney Crabb, #3333: AQS, 1993, 360 pages, 5½ x 8½, softbound, $14.95
- **Quilt Groups Today: Who They Are, Where They Meet, What They Do, and How to Contact Them – A Complete Guide for 1992-1993,** #3308: AQS, 1992, 336 pages, softbound, $14.95
- **Quilt Registry,** Lynne Fritz, #2380: AQS, 1992, 80 pages, hardbound, $9.95
- **Quilting Patterns from Native American Designs,** Dr. Joyce Mori, #3467: AQS, 1993, 80 pages, softbound, $12.95
- **Quilting with Style: Principles for Great Pattern Design,** Gwen Marston & Joe Cunningham, #3470: AQS, 1993, 192 pages, 9 x 12, hardbound, $24.95
- **Quiltmaker's Guide: Basics & Beyond,** Carol Doak, #2284: AQS, 1992, 208 pages, softbound, $19.95
- **Quilts: Old & New, A Similar View,** Paul D. Pilgrim and Gerald E. Roy, #3715: AQS, 1993, 40 pages, softbound, $12.95
- **Quilts: The Permanent Collection – MAQS,** #2257: AQS, 1991, 100 pages, 10 x 6½, softbound, $9.95
- **Seasons of the Heart & Home: Quilts for a Winter's Day,** Jan Patek, #3796: AQS, 1993, 160 pages, softbound, $18.95
- **Seasons of the Heart & Home: Quilts for Summer Days,** Jan Patek, #3761: AQS, 1993, 160 pages, softbound, $18.95
- **Sensational Scrap Quilts,** Darra Duffy Williamson, #2357: AQS, 1992, 152 pages, softbound, $24.95
- **Sets & Borders,** Gwen Marston & Joe Cunningham, #1821: AQS, 1987, 104 pages, softbound, $14.95
- **Show Me Helen...How to Use Quilting Designs,** Helen Squire, #3375: AQS, 1993, 155 pages, softbound, $15.95
- **Somewhere in Between: Quilts and Quilters of Illinois,** Rita Barrow Barber, #1790: AQS, 1986, 78 pages, softbound, $14.95
- **Spike & Zola: Patterns for Laughter...and Appliqué, Painting, or Stenciling,** Donna French Collins, #3794: AQS, 1993, 72 pages, softbound, $9.95
- **Stenciled Quilts for Christmas,** Marie Monteith Sturmer, #2098: AQS, 1990, 104 pages, softbound, $14.95
- **Three-Dimensional Appliqué and Embroidery Embellishment: Techniques for Today's Album Quilt,** Anita Shackelford, #3788: AQS, 1993, 152 pages, 9 x 12, hardbound, $24.95
- **A Treasury of Quilting Designs,** Linda Goodmon Emery, #2029: AQS, 1990, 80 pages, 14 x 11, spiral-bound, $14.95
- **Tricks with Chintz: Using Large Prints to Add New Magic to Traditional Quilt Blocks,** Nancy S. Breland, #3847: AQS, 1994, 96 pages, softbound, $14.95
- **Wonderful Wearables: A Celebration of Creative Clothing,** Virginia Avery, #2286: AQS, 1991, 184 pages, softbound, $24.95

These books can be found in local bookstores and quilt shops. If you are unable to locate a title in your area, you can order by mail from AQS, P.O. Box 3290, Paducah, KY 42002-3290.
Please add $1 for the first book and 40¢ for each additional one to cover postage and handling.
(International orders please add $1.50 for the first book and $1 for each additional one.)